Investing in
Junk Bonds

Investing in Junk Bonds

INSIDE
THE
HIGH YIELD
DEBT
MARKET

BY EDWARD I. ALTMAN AND
SCOTT A. NAMMACHER

BeardBooks
Washington, DC

Library of Congress Cataloging-in-Publication Data

Altman, Edward I., 1941-
    Investing in junk bonds : inside the high yield debt marker / Edward I. Altman,
Scott A. Nammacher.
        p. cm.
    Originally published: New york : Wiley, c1987, in series: Wiley professional banking
and finance series.
    Includes bibliographical references and index.
    ISBN 1-58798-155-6
        1. Junk bonds. I Nammacher, Scott A. II. Title.

HD4651 .A63 2002
332.63'234--dc21

                                                                          2002033273

Preface

In less than a decade, the high yield "junk" bond market has catapulted from an insignificant, negative element in the corporate fixed income market to one of the fastest growing and most controversial segments of all investment vehicles. The term "junk" emanates from the dominant high yield bond issues prior to 1978 when the market was almost entirely made up of original issue investment grade securities that fell from their lofty credit status to a high risk, speculative grade. Currently, the proportion of original issue, investment grade debt is somewhere between 20 and 30% of the market and the original issue junk bond segment comprises about 15% of total corporate new issue debt.

The purpose of this book is to provide market participants and other interested observers with an in-depth look at the high yield debt sector, both past and present. Current and prospective investors in speculative grade debt will find the content particularly relevant as much of it relates to the market's size, growth, default rate, and return, along with discussions on various relevant investment strategies.

Investors, whether professional managers of mutual, pension, or trust funds and special investment groups or individuals investing for their own accounts, must clearly understand the market's risks and returns relative to other investment types in order to develop specific investment strategies.

Among the topics discussed in this book are expected yields, realized returns, default experience, market growth and size, credit quality trends, related mutual fund results and portfolio holdings, mergers/acquisitions and takeovers, new issue and issuer characteristics, underwriter standings, investment strategies using an objective credit model, and much more.

Will an intimate knowledge of these topics guarantee the investor success in junk bonds? Obviously not. Historical experience, particularly when the financial system undergoes extensive change or realignment, is not necessarily a strong predictor of the future, particularly with respect to absolute return levels. The 1978 to 1985 period studied here includes years when absolute yields and returns reached record levels. During the latter part of our study period, comparative return levels dropped substantially. On the positive side, given the results documented over time by various researchers (for example, Hickman, Atkinson, etc.) indicating substantial yield and return spreads on low-rated debt well in excess of investment grade issues, even after adjustment for defaults, we feel this marketplace will continue to yield significant premium returns for some years to come.

How can individual investors with limited funds best enter this market? We would recommend investing through mutual funds. They allow the small investor maximum diversification (protection from individual defaults or credit downgrades) and in most cases, very reasonable returns. The high yield sector offers attractive opportunities but is not a market for the layperson to invest in directly. For the professional fund manager or sophisticated analyst, we present certain credit analysis techniques to aid in selecting among the more than 500 issuers and over 1100 issues that made up the marketplace at year end 1985. Chapter 1 is an introduction to the high yield debt market. Chapter 2 examines the anatomy of the high yield debt market, its size, growth, yield and return experience over the last 10 years. New issuer characteristics and the underwriter's role are discussed in Chapter 3. This chapter also includes a brief analysis of the construction of models for estimating the underwriting fee (spread) on high yield debt. In Chapter 4, we discuss the factors that led to the great increase in investor interest in this market. In addition, we will assess the role and characteristics of high yield debt mutual funds as well as other financial intermediaries.

A critical question is the default risk on these non-investment grade bonds. Chapter 5 presents a comprehensive study on the default rate experience on high yield debt—indeed all corporate debt—over the last 15 years. After measuring default, Chapter 6 explores a relatively new tool for avoiding it—the Zeta® score approach. In addition to its use for investment purposes, we examine Zeta to measure changes in overall credit quality in this rapidly expanding market. Next, Chapter 7 will explore the subject of mergers and acquisitions and high yield debt's role in this controversial area. The final two chapters, 8 and 9, explore portfolio measures and strategies for the high yield market, reflecting active as well as passive investment techniques.

We drew heavily on our research which has been generously sponsored by the Fixed Income Research Department of Morgan Stanley & Co., Incorporated. Several of our reports, published by Morgan Stanley for their clients and other interested parties, form the nucleus of our material and we are grateful for that firm's support and enthusiasm for the project. In particular, we would like to express our appreciation to Robert Platt, Director of Fixed Income Research, and Martin Fridson, editor of *High Performance*, for their encouragement and to the firm of Morgan Stanley & Co., Incorporated for giving permission to use our published materials in this volume. Also at Morgan Stanley, the technical assistance of James Lucas, Michael Marocco, Fritz Wahl, and Lorraine McCorry is gratefully acknowledged. From the investment banking firm of Drexel Burnham Lambert, we would like to thank Larry Post, editor of the *High Yield Newsletter,* for providing us with valuable information. Henry Schilling of Lipper Analytical Securities Corp. in New York and Gail Hessol of Standard & Poor's also provided timely data. We hasten to add, however, that the results and conclusions are ours alone and do not necessarily reflect the opinions of any of these institutions or individuals.

There were a large number of other people who assisted us in our work. To name them all is impossible, but we would like to single out several graduate assistants from NYU's Graduate Business School including Nayan Kisnadwala, Jeffrey Klearman, Susan Meah, and Evan Wan. Research, so data oriented, could not be efficiently processed without such invaluable help. Diana Coryat, Alice Markowski, and especially Teresa Santamaria provided indispensable typing and editing support. Finally to our wives, Elaine and Bonnie, we owe our gratitude for putting up with such an unattractive name as "junk" and for accepting it as part of our everyday vocabulary.

EDWARD I. ALTMAN
SCOTT A. NAMMACHER

New York, New York
October 1986

Contents

1
Introducing the High Yield Debt Market

HIGH YIELD DEBT—WHAT IS IT?

In recent years the level of new, public, nonconvertible corporate debt issued annually in the United States has risen dramatically, from $22.4 billion in 1978 to over $101 billion in 1985. While the majority of this expansion occurred as a result of falling interest rates in 1984 and 1985, a significant portion of the growth came from a previously undeveloped subcategory of the marketplace, that of high yield bonds.

High yield or "junk" bonds (also referred to as speculative grade, low-rated, or noninvestment grade bonds) are generally defined as publicly traded debt obligations rated as noninvestment grade by at least one of the independent rating agencies. More specifically, they include securities rated below BBB- (Standard & Poor's) or Baa3 (Moody's), that is, BB or Ba, B, CCC or Caa down to D (default), and certain nonrated securities that may or may not be tracked by the major rating agencies. The nonrated sector generally includes those bonds with promised yields that are within the range of those observed on rated, high yield debt. For those readers who are unfamiliar with debt ratings, basically, the higher the rating the lower the risk of default on either principal or interest payments (triple-A being the highest grade and D being in default).

Debt in the high yield corporate sector carries a very real level of speculative risk, and as a result, investors have demanded yield premiums to compensate for that risk. Over the last decade, these securities have usually sold with yield spreads (or risk premiums) of between 2.5 and 5.0% over comparable long-term government securities. These premiums and the rising interest rates in the late 1970s and early 1980s were major factors in the rapid expansion of the high yield bond marketplace. Before going further, we should identify the specific parts of the "junk" marketplace that we will be referring to throughout the book.

Securities in both the high yield and investment grade sectors can be broken down into several major types of debt (none of which is mutually exclusive), including fixed and variable rate issues, convertible securities, zero coupon bonds and debt with warrants, stock or other types of "kickers" (usually called unit offerings and found mostly in the high yield sector). In addition, debt issues can also be subdivided by the nature of the offering itself, into categories that include fully underwritten primary offerings, "best efforts" offerings, exchange offerings, and secondary offerings.

In this book, we concentrate almost solely on high yield, nonconvertible, corporate industrial, finance, and utility securities that are rated by at least one of the rating agencies as below investment grade. We excluded (except where noted) exchange, "best efforts," and secondary offerings in our new issue statistics because either the issue amounts were extremely difficult to verify or the offering revenues did not flow back to the issuer itself.

The last decade or so has seen enormous growth in this market in terms of the number of new issues and dollar amounts outstanding. For example, in 1976 there was approximately $8 billion of high yield nonconvertible, debt outstanding with the average individual issue being $27 million. This amount grew slowly but steadily for the next few years until 1980 when the market jumped to over $15 billion, up from $10.7 billion in 1979. Since 1982, the high yield market has exploded and by mid-1986, it totaled almost $93 billion in *rated, nonconvertible* (or *"straight"*) *debt securities* comprising over 16% of the public straight debt outstanding, up from just under 6.0% in 1982.

Some analysts estimate that another 10 to 15% should be added to these figures to account for nonrated debt securities which have similar characteristics but are not followed by the major rating agencies. If one includes these issues plus convertible debt, certain types of preferred stocks and publicly traded, higher risk municipals, the total high yield public market was well in excess of $100 billion.

Newly issued, straight debt in 1985 amounted to $14.7 billion (net of exchange, secondary, and "best efforts" offerings, and retirements). In 1985, these new issues accounted for 14.5% of all new corporate/utility, publicly issued straight debt. If you include all types of low-rated debt (exchange offers, retirements, etc.), the high yield component approached 20% of the total newly issued corporate debt. Clearly, this speculative grade debt segment has grown to be an important part of the debt marketplace.

WHY IS IT CALLED JUNK?

In our society the term "junk" automatically connotes some negative quality to the item being evaluated. Hence, we hear the terms "junk-yard," "junk-food," or just plain "junk" to identify inferior goods, and so it goes for financial securities as well, much to the chagrin of those who participate in this market—issuing companies, underwriters, traders, and investors. Perhaps the primary beneficiaries of the term junk are those media and other observers who follow and report on this increasingly important segment of the debt market. In addition, intense emotion is conjured up by critics when they refer to those debt securities that are helping to fuel hostile takeovers of U.S. corporations by so-called fast-buck corporate raiders. Other, less emotional critics are concerned with the credit quality of these junk bonds, especially since the market is much larger today than it was just a few years ago. One of our objectives is to provide an unemotional picture of this market.

The term junk originated in the mid-1970s to describe those corporate securities that lost their investment grade status due to a fundamental deterioration in the quality of their operating and financial performance. These so-called "fallen angels" involved both industrial and public utility debt where the default probability was considered sufficiently high so as to drop the bonds from the list of investment grade securities.

Since the late 1970s, the proportion of high yield debt made up of fallen angels has diminished through mid-1985 to about 29% but jumped somewhat higher by year end due mostly to two very large additions, Texaco and Union Carbide. The market began to include more newly issued or original issue debt that represented a source of capital for emerging or continuing growth companies, and those other companies which previously relied solely on private placements (i.e., commercial bank debt or debt placed directly with other institutional investors such as insurance companies). As privately placed debt typically has rigid debt indenture provisions, restricting a firm's financial and operating flexibility to protect a specific lender's interest, many corporate treasurers have been willing to utilize the less restrictive public high yield market.

Corporate raiders, on the other hand, viewed this new found source of (relatively) restriction-free debt as an effective tool for financing hostile takeovers of firms, usually much larger in asset size than their own. A relatively small number of well publicized takeover battles in 1984 and 1985 has turned the use of junk bonds for acquisitions into an emotionally charged topic of debate. We will return to this issue in Chapter 7.

WHY HAS THIS MARKET GROWN AND WHO'S INVOLVED?

Rising interest rates and rapid expansion of the supply of high yield corporate debt since the late 1970s led a wide variety of financial institutions to explore the relative attractions of lower-rated debt securities. Investors in investment grade and even "risk-free" government securities were increasingly disenchanted with low or negative *expost* returns on their portfolios as interest rates rose and prices declined. Committed to fixed income investment, especially because equity returns were not much better or worse in some periods, these investors began to "eye" the high coupon debt securities found in the junk-yard. In addition to the observed superior yields, the high yield sector offered increased liquidity and diversification potential over what it had just a few short years before.

The entire high yield, straight debt market at the beginning of 1986 was comprised of over 500 different corporate issuers and had over 1100 debt issues available to choose from. Of course, many of these issues were small, that is, under $25 million in debt outstanding, with an actual floating or tradeable supply even lower. Still, the number of rated, new issues greater than $200 million in size was 20 in 1984 and 23 in 1985. There were a substantially larger number of issues greater than $100 million in these years, as well.

The major players in the high yield debt "game" are (1) issuing companies, (2) investors, (3) underwriting investment bankers, and (4) rating agencies. These are the same participants as found in the investment grade segment of the debt market. An increasingly important external constituency has emerged recently, made up of various observer/regulator type groups, including financial institution regulators, congressional committees, the media, and a small number of researchers. Investor interest in this emerging field is perhaps best exemplified by the growth in the number of mutual funds in the area, from less than a dozen 10 years ago to 44 as of June 1986. As of June 30, 1986, they had a total net asset value in excess of $20 billion. Interest from the investment banking community has also grown to the extent that competition for new issue underwriting has been active.

Drexel Burnham Lambert, by far the leader and driving force behind the high yield field, devotes several hundred people to analyzing, underwriting, trading, and writing about high yield bonds. Their dominance of the field in 1984 made them the number two corporate debt underwriter for the year, second only to Salomon Brothers, Inc. Only recently have other major investment banks made concerted efforts to jump on the "junk-wagon." High investor interest and lucrative underwriting spreads (fees) will likely cause investment banks to devote additional resources to the area, thereby spurring greater growth and diversification in the near future.

In terms of credit research, Standard & Poor's has started a separate department to concentrate on high yield bonds while Moody's has begun to issue regular credit reports on below investment grade bonds. Investment banks have also moved aggressively into this area, with many establishing special credit and research areas, internally, to evaluate and report on potential offerings, trading opportunities and market trends. Morgan Stanley & Co., Incorporated publishes a monthly magazine, *High Performance*, and Drexel Burnham Lambert publishes *High Yield Newsletter* bimonthly.

RECENT ISSUES AND REGULATIONS

High yield bonds have attracted a great deal of attention recently from Congress and government regulators. Their primary concerns have revolved around two issues—the use of junk bonds in highly leveraged hostile takeovers and the exposure of federally insured savings and loan associations to the default risks (and potential losses) thought to be inherent in high yield junk bonds.

To date, the primary result of their attention has been the January 1986 controversial decision by the Federal Reserve Bank's (Fed) Board of Governors to apply federally regulated margin requirements, Regulation G, to certain types of highly leveraged acquisitions. Their action limits a hostile acquiror's ability to issue high yield bonds in order to fund a takeover where the debt is effectively supported by the income from the acquired firm's assets. The Fed, in effect, limited the debt that can be guaranteed by the acquiree's income to 50% of the purchase price. Security for the remaining debt must come from the acquiror. (See Chapter 7 for details.) The argument put forward is that since certain merger financing is secured only by the asset value of the target company—and by extension the equity value of that firm, then it is in essence an equity financed venture and therefore is subject to the usual equity margin requirements.

In an unusual display of public criticism of the Fed, a number of federal agencies including the Justice Department, the Treasury Department, and the Securities and Exchange Commission came out strongly against the margin requirement as they felt it was inconsistent with an open, free wheeling, capitalistic marketplace and would help stifle the economy's growth. Critics of the Fed's action see their move, not so much as a safeguard against takeover abuses, but as the first step in a continuing process of federal regulation and psychological fallout against high yield junk financings.

Many analysts and legal experts, however, predict that the regulation's impact on takeover attempts will be limited, as other creative financial arrangements are made to substitute for the pure, junk debt acquisition play. If nothing else, the new regulation will cause existing and prospective acquirors to reassess their strategies. The debate over whether high yield bonds should be used by federally insured banking institutions will be discussed in Chapter 4.

OBJECTIVES AND RECOMMENDATIONS

Basically, we have attempted to present an indepth anatomy of the key elements of this market as they relate to its investors (primarily) in a detailed form that enables players to dissect and customize the data for additional internal analyses.

A key part of our overall objective has been to quantify the recent risk/return relationship in a manner that gives the investor (large or small) the information necessary to evaluate and develop an appropriate high yield debt investment strategy.

The results of our study indicate that over the last decade junk bonds offered a very attractive return-vesus-risk tradeoff for investors. Not only have prudent investors done well relative to other fixed income opportunities, but this market has provided an important source of funds for emerging growth companies (as well as fees for their investment bankers and advisors).

The default rate, which remained relatively low on average from 1974 to 1985, has and will continue to fluctuate widely from one year to the next, particularly in recessionary years. This variability can cause substantial losses for unsophisticated and/or undiversified investors. For this reason, we strongly believe the small, individual investor wishing to participate should do so via professionally managed mutual funds. We have included a list of the major ones along with details on fees, holdings, historical returns, phone numbers, etc. to facilitate the gathering of information from funds of interest.

For the larger, institutional investor with access to professional credit analysts and the funds to enable adequate diversification, we present the results of testing various credit strategies designed to reduce default risk yet maintain superior returns. Here, we found that an objective multivariate credit model can reduce the investor's exposure to defaults without significantly effecting portfolio returns. Such a model combined with additional qualitative analyses by knowledgeable credit analysts should minimize investor exposure to high risk issuers.

We recommend, regardless of investment size, that interested players place their funds in a diversified group of creditworthy companies selected on the basis of a specific investment objective. While no one can predict the future of this marketplace, particularly during recessionary times, we feel it will continue to grow as more companies and investors enter the arena. In the final analysis, with sound credit assessments, diversification, and a degree of investor prudence, the high yield marketplace can be an attractive junk yard to "play" in.

2

The Anatomy of the High Yield Debt Market

GROWTH OF THE MARKET

Rising interest rates and rapid expansion of the high yield corporate debt market since the late 1970s have led a wide variety of financial institutions to explore the relative attractions of lower-rated securities. In addition to the promised superior yields and realized impressive returns, the high yield sector now offers considerable liquidity and diversification potential. It has been estimated that total outstanding debt in this area was over $100 billion by the end of 1985. The segment analyzed in this chapter, *all low-rated, public, nonconvertible debt*, grew from under $8 billion in 1978 to almost $42 billion in 1984, was almost $60 billion by mid-1985 and $93 billion by mid-1986. Estimates from individuals dealing in these markets indicate that an additional 10 to 15% of the rated debt market can be found in *nonrated* high yield securities. In 1984 and again in 1985, nearly $15 billion in new straight high yield financing was issued and if one includes exchange and best efforts offers plus secondary issues, the total exceeded $19 billion in 1985. Given the market's size, growth rate, yield, and capital raising potential, it has become an increasingly important area. In this chapter we detail the anatomy of the publicly traded, straight (nonconvertible), high yield bond market.

INTEREST RATES AND RETURNS

The period from 1978 to 1985 was an exceptionally volatile one for interest rates and corporate profitability. Interest rates on 3 month T-bills and on 10 year government bonds rose from 7.4% and 8.4% yield levels respectively in early 1978, to record heights, peaking in mid-1981 at 17.2% and 15.3% respectively. By the fourth quarter of 1982, T-bills had dropped to 8% while 10 year government bonds were near the 10.5% level (see Exhibit 2-1). At the same time, corporate profits plummeted in the 1981–1982 recession and

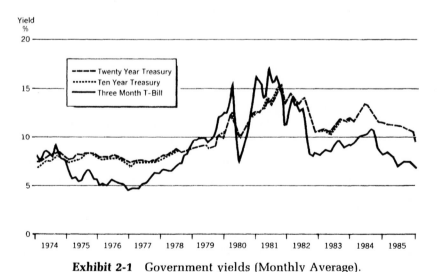

Exhibit 2-1   Government yields (Monthly Average).

bankruptcies reached record postdepression levels. Despite the overall economy's expansion from 1983 to 1985, the number of business failures and corporate distress situations has remained at historically high levels.

This volatility caused large variations in bond returns and yields over the period. Investment managers holding a portfolio equivalent to the Shearson Lehman Long-Term Government Bond Index would have experienced losses or marginally positive returns for all but three (1982, 1984, and 1985) years of the eight-year period from 1978 through 1985 (Table 2-1). In effect, rising interest rates caused substantial reductions in the market value of their holdings, more than offsetting the coupon income these bonds generated. The decline in rates in 1982 and 1985 saved investors in long-term government bonds from having a very low return over the entire period.

With high quality bond returns fluctuating at or below zero returns from 1978 through 1981, portfolio managers began looking for new opportunities to boost their returns. High yield bonds from 1978 to 1981 returned an average of 4.4% on investment while long-term government bonds returned an average of −1.1%. (The source of our high yield returns was a Morgan Stanley database constructed by the authors.) The high yield bond marketplace became an increasingly attractive option.

Results from our data base indicate that investors in high yield bonds from December 31, 1977 to December 31, 1983 (the last full calendar year of our database) would have realized a compounded return of 11.45% versus 5.62% for long-term government bonds, a 583 basis point difference annually. Returns are very sensitive to the time period examined, however. For example, the return spread for the period March 31, 1978 to March 31, 1984 was 490 basis points. A three month shift caused a 93 point change in

Table 2-1. Annual Returns, Yields and Spreads on Long-Term (LT) Government Bonds and High Yield (HY) Bonds (Calendar Years)

Year	Return HY[a]	Return LT Gov't[b]	Return Spread	Promised Yield[c] HY	Promised Yield[c] LT Gov't	Promised Yield[c] Spread
1978	7.57%	−1.11%	8.68%	10.92%	8.11%	2.81%
1979	3.69	−0.86	4.55	12.07	9.13	2.94
1980	−1.00	−2.96	1.96	13.46	10.23	3.23
1981	7.56	0.48	7.08	15.97	12.08	3.89
1982	32.45	42.08	−9.63	17.84	13.86	3.98
1983	21.80	2.23	19.57	15.74	10.70	5.04
1984	8.50[d]	14.82	−6.32	14.97	11.87	3.10
1985	22.51[d]	31.54	−9.03	15.40[d]	11.65	3.75
1986	n.a.	n.a.	n.a.	14.45[d]	9.55	4.90
Arithmetic averages						
1978 to 1983	12.01	6.64	5.37	14.33	10.68	3.65
1978 to 1985	12.89	10.78	2.11	14.55	10.95	3.60
1978 to 1986	n.a.	n.a.	n.a.	14.54	10.80	3.74
Compounded averages						
1978 to 1983	11.45	5.62	5.83			
1978 to 1985	12.40	9.70	2.70			

[a] Morgan Stanley composite generated from over 440 high yield issues. Actual portfolio ranged in size from 153 in 1978 to 339 issues in 1983. This data base goes through March 31, 1984.

[b] Shearson Lehman Long-Term Government Bond Index.

[c] Promised yield as of beginning of year. It represents the internal rate of return based on the security's current price and scheduled payments of interest and principal.

[d] Drexel Burnham Lambert Composite Index, from High Yield Newsletter. Note this index does not include reinvested coupon payments and differs somewhat from the 1978 to 1983 measures. Yield spreads do not include CCC (Caa) debt.

returns. That differential narrowed to 270 basis points by the end of 1985. The *arithmetic average annual return spread* was 211 basis points, or 2.11% at the end of 1985, 370 basis points at the end of 1984 versus 5.37% or 537 base points at the end of 1983. The average yield spread between high yield bonds and long-term governments over the same time frame (measured annually on the first trading day of each year) was 365 basis points (BP) through the beginning of 1983, 360 BP through the beginning of 1985 and 374 BP through the start of 1986. Selected annual returns and yields are displayed in Table 2-1 and Exhibit 2-2. It is interesting to note that the average yield spread (exante) and average return spread (expost) from 1978 to 1984 were actually similar (3.57% vs. 3.70%) but there is very little similarity for each specific year. The differential was somewhat greater (149 BP) over the period 1978 to 1985 (360 v. 211).

Another way of measuring returns of different bond portfolios is to observe the performance of various types of mutual funds. Exhibits 2-3a and 2-3b highlight the mutual bond fund performance of a number of strategies over the period 1975 to 1985 and for 1984 and 1985 alone. These statistics were compiled by Lipper Analytical Services and represent the average reinvested return performance of a number of funds investing in each category. Note that the return performance for the 10-year period is consistent with perceived risk attributes. The highest yielding funds were those of the High Current Yield category followed by General Bonds, Triple-B, Single-A, and U.S. Governments categories. Our own database calculations for the period April 1978 to April 1984 show the same relative rankings as the Lipper rankings. We should point out that the Lipper data on High Current Yield Funds are not strictly based on high yield securities, since these portfolios also include some investment grade and government debt. We will return to this factor in Chapter 4.

In 1984, high yield bond funds recorded only a 7.23%

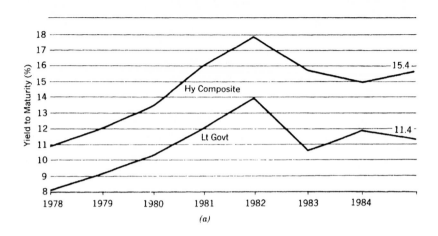

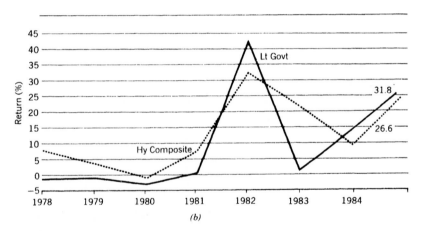

Exhibit 2-2   (a) Calendar year yields at the beginning of each year,
(b) Calendar year returns 1978 through 1984.

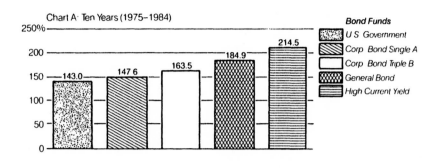

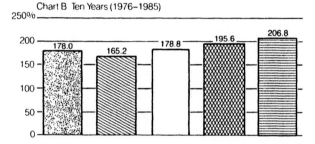

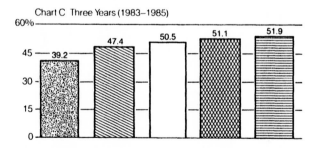

Source Lipper Analytical Services, Inc

Exhibit 2-3a Selected groups of long-term taxable bond funds: total reinvested returns for 3 and 10 year periods.

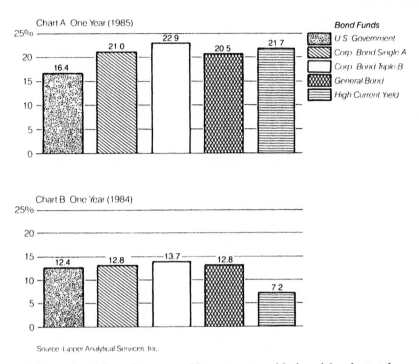

Exhibit 2-3b   Selected groups of long-term taxable bond funds: total reinvested returns for one year periods 1984 and 1985.

return compared to over 12% for all other fixed income categories. In 1985, the High Current Yield Funds' average surpassed all but the Triple-B group. Note the fixed income groups of securities will experience different returns depending on the maturity horizon and duration of the particular portfolio. For example, some very long-term government bond indexes realized returns in excess of 30% in 1985. Only time will tell whether or not the 1984 and 1985 results are typical of expected return spreads between different fixed income strategies. We believe, however, that the risk-reward tradeoff among different quality issues will be, in all likelihood, well reflected in actual returns over the long run.

Exhibit 2-4 presents the monthly index of returns for our composite of high yield bonds. Monthly returns varied from a high of 13.3% in April 1980 to a low of −7.61% in October 1979. The average over the primary study period March 31, 1978 to March 31, 1984 was 0.92% per month. Long-term government bonds had their highs and lows in the same months as the high yield bonds and averaged 0.52% per month over the same period. Premiums like these are a major reason that demand in the high yield market expanded so rapidly. We will discuss monthly and annual returns in greater depth in Chapters 8 and 9.

SIZE AND GROWTH IN HIGH YIELD DEBT

Table 2-2 shows how quickly the market size has changed. In 1978 the par value of public low-rated straight debt out-

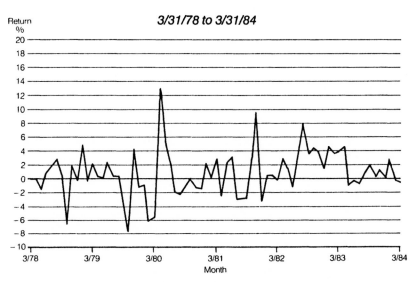

Exhibit 2-4 Monthly returns for HY composite.

Table 2-2. Public Straight Debt Outstanding 1970 to 1985 ($MM)

Year	Par Value Public Straight Debt Outstanding Over Year[b]	Straight Public Debt[c]	Low Rated Debt[a]		
			Percent of Public Straight Debt	Amount Outstanding Per Issuer	Amount Outstanding Per Issue
1985	$395,500(est.)	$59,078	14.9	$135	$55
1984	363,300	41,700	11.5	125	49
1983	339,850	28,223	8.3	93	39
1982	320,850	18,536	5.8	69	33
1981	303,800	17,362	5.7	62	32
1980	282,000	15,125	5.4	59	31
1979	260,600	10,675	4.1	47	30
1978	245,000	9,401	3.8	49	30
1977	228,500	8,479	3.7	46	27
1976	209,900	8,015	3.8	41	27
1975	187,900	7,720	4.1	41	27
1974	167,000	11,101[d]	6.6	59	35
1973	154,800[e]	8,082	5.2	45	29
1972	145,700	7,106	4.9	45	29
1971	132,500	6,643	5.0	45	29
1970	116,200	6,996	6.0	48	32

[a] Source: Standard & Poor's Bond Guide and Moody's Bond Record, July issues of each year. Defaulted railroads excluded. Also includes nonrated debt equivalent to rated debt for low-rated firms.

[b] Average of beginning and ending years' figures (1975–1985).

[c] Includes high yield exchange debt.

[d] Includes $2.7 billion in Con Edison debt.

[e] Estimates for 1973 and earlier based on linear regression of this column versus the Federal Reserve's Corporate Bonds Outstanding figures (Federal Reserve Bulletin.)

standing represented 3.8% of the total public straight debt outstanding. By 1985 low-rated debt had grown to represent 13% of the corporate debt market. Total public straight debt outstanding grew 61% from 1978 to 1985. High yield, rated public debt more than quintupled, from $9 billion to over $59 billion (including over $8 billion in exchange debt). At the same time, the amount of debt per company and per issue grew substantially. The debt per company grew from $49 million to $135 million and the average outstanding per issue grew from $30 million to $55 million by 1985 in just seven years.

NEW ISSUES 1978–1984

The *new* issue public, straight debt marketplace (see Table 2-3) has grown phenomenally, moving from the $1.5 billion level in 1978 to just under $15 billion in 1984. The latter figure represents a 100% increase over 1983. (The totals do not include exchange offers, best effort offerings, convertibles, or secondary offerings of existing debt.) The high yield marketplace represented 15% of 1984's new straight corporate debt issues. New issue business in 1984 alone accounted for over 48% of the total new issue business in the high yield marketplace since 1978 with a record number of issues $200 million (par value) or more. Table 2-4a,b lists these issues (20), up from only 6 the year before. The number of deals $100 million or larger rose from 2 in 1978 to 23 in 1983 and to 58 in 1984 (representing over 46% of the issues done in 1984, up from 27% in 1983). These figures do not include "best efforts" offerings. Between 1978 and 1984 there were 21 CCC rated, 256 B rated, 96 BB rated and 13 BBB/Ba rated new issues. The B and CCC rated issues ac-

Table 2-3. New Nonconvertible Domestic Debt Issues: 1978 to 1985 ($MM)

Year	Total Par Value New Issues Public Straight Debt		Total New Par Value High Yield Debt Issues[a]		Percent New Issue Dollars	Issued with Warrants or Stock	Variable Rate Debt	
	Amount	Number	Amount	Number	Percent	Number	Amount	Number
1985[a]	$101,098	1212	$14,670	188	14.5	18	$2,543	12
1984	99,416	721	14,952	124	15.0	18	3,927	27
1983	46,903	511	7,417	86	15.8	35	—	—
1982	47,798	513	2,798	48	5.9	10	40	1
1981	41,651	357	1,648	32	4.0	6	104	2
1980	37,272	398	1,442	43	3.9	8	137	4
1979	25,678	277	1,307	45	5.0	14	—	—
1978	22,416	287	1,493	52	6.7	15	—	—
Total	$423,536	4284	$45,757	618	10.8	124	$6,751	46

Source: Morgan Stanley & Co., Incorporated

[a] Not including exchange offers, secondary offerings, tax exempts, convertibles or government agencies. In 1985, exchange offers and reorganization issues totaled $3.96 billion; Retirements were $1.62 billion and secondary issues were at least $1.1 billion.

Table 2-4a. 1984 New Straight Debt Issues of \$200 Million or More (Par Value, \$MM)[a]

Issuer	Coupon	Maturity	Par Value	Rating[b]
Occidental Petroleum	9.65s	1994	$1,200	BB –
Occidental Petroleum	8.95s	1994	700	BBB/Ba3
Coastal Corp., Houston	VRN	1994	600	BB –
Rapid American	Os	1985–2007	506	CCC
Mesa Petroleum	VRN	1994	500	BB –
ACF Industries	15.25s	1996	400	BBB/Ba3
Metromedia Broadcasting	Adj. rate	2002	400	B –
Occidental Petroleum	VRN	1994	350	BBB/Ba3
Metromedia Broadcasting	VRN	1996	335	B +
Middle South Energy	16.0s	2000	300	BB –
Chrysler Financial	VRN	1992	300	B
Metromedia Broadcasting	15.625s	1999	225	B –
Chrysler Financial	13.5s	1991	200	B
Chrysler Financial	VRN	1994	200	B
Chrysler Financial	12.75s	1999	200	BB –
Chrysler Financial	13.25s	1999	200	BB –
I.C.H. Corp.	16.5s	1994	200	BB –
Rapid American	14.5s	1994	200	CCC
Resorts International	16.25s	2004	200	B +
Turner Broadcasting	12.875s	1994	200	B –

Source: Morgan Stanley & Co., Incorporated.
[a] Not including best effort offerings. Note: two large issues (Metromedia O's 1998 and Harte-Hanks Comm. O's 2004) were not listed because their final issue amounts could not be verified.
[b] Moody's rating indicated when its rating differed from S&P's investment grade.

Table 2-4*b*. 1985 New Straight Debt Issues of $200MM or More (Par Value, $MM)[a]

Issuer	Coupon	Maturity	Par Value	Rating (S&P/Moody's)
SCI Holdings (3 issues)	0	1990 to 1995	1200	B/Ba3
Phillips Petroleum	14¾	2000	1100	BBB – /Bal (Exchange)
SCI Holdings	15	1997	608	CCC/B2
LTV	7⅞	1998	560	Exchange
Sharon Steel	13½	2000	426	Exchange
Multimedia	0–16	2005	400	Exchange
Levi-Strauss Associates	14.45	2000	375	B – /B1
Stone Container	13⅝	1995	350	BB – /B1
Minstar	14⅞	1995	300	NR/B3
Wickes Cos.	15	1995	299	CCC/B3 (Reorg.)
Golden Nugget Finance	13¼	1995	260	BB – /NR
Pantry Pride	14⅜	1997	259	CCC/B3
Chrysler Finance	Floating	1995	250	BBB – /Ba2
Nortek	13½	1997	250	B/B1
Dart Group	14	1995	250	B + /B1
Long Island Lighting	13¼	1997	225	B/B1
Pantry Pride	Variable	1997	225	CCC/B3
Chicago Pacific	14	1995	200	B – /B2
Las Colinas	12½	1992	200	NR/Ba2
Harte-Hanks Communications	13⅞	1995	200	B – /B1
Harte-Hanks Communications	14⅜	2000	200	B – /B1

[a] Does not include NR for Both Moody's and S&P except for exchange debt where indicated. At least two additional issues were nonrated.

counted for over 62% of the high yield debt issues and 53% of the new high yield issue dollars in 1984.

The average issue size changed over the years, from $28 million in 1978 to over $120 million in 1984 (see Table 2-5). The median issue in 1984 was $77 million. That year saw both record size issues (i.e., Metromedia—$1.3 billion raised using a complex combination of four types of securities) and a record number of offerings (124, up by 44% over the prior year). We will see in the next secton that both the average and median size of new issues dropped considerably in 1985 although the number of issues increased significantly.

The average "years to maturity" of new issues dropped as interest rates increased. In 1978, the average life was 19 years (ignoring sinking funds). By 1984 it had fallen to 12 years. The average "duration" of bonds in our high yield universe was 6.45 years in 1983, down from 7.87 years in 1978, and has averaged 6.64 years over the six-year period. By contrast, the average duration of Shearson Lehman's Long-Term Government Bond Index over the same period was 8.53 years. The concept of duration is important for performance evaluation. For a description of its meaning and calculation, see Appendix 3 and a more in-depth discussion in Chapters 8 and 9. See Table 2-6 for yield and duration attributes of various portfolios. In 1984 and 1985, despite interest rates moving in a downward trend, issuers have continued to shorten the years to maturity and duration on their debt.

1985: A RECORD NEW ISSUE YEAR?
YES AND NO

In aggregate dollars, 1985 was indeed a record year for newly issued high yield bonds, with almost $20 billion offered to the public. The new straight debt issued (Table 2-3)

Table 2-5. Public High Yield New Issue Statistics[a]

Year	S&P Rating[b]	Total Amount Issued ($M)	Number of Issues	Average Years to Maturity	Average Issue Amount ($M)
1985	BBB/Ba	$ 1,065,000	11	10	$ 96,818
	BB	2,040,750	23	11	88,728
	B	6,038,033	77	11	78,416
	CCC	1,668,000	14	11	119,143
	No Rating	3,858,641	63	11	61,248
Total:		14,670,424	188	11	78,034
1984	BBB/Ba	1,290,000	5	9	258,000
	BB	4,698,000	23	13	204,260
	B	6,484,500	68	11	95,360
	CCC	1,476,000	9	12	164,000
	No Rating	1,003,469	19	13	52,814
Total:		14,951,969	124	12	120,580
1983	BBB/Ba	—	—	—	
	BB	2,893,738	24	17	120,572
	B	3,713,451	46	14	80,727
	CCC	285,000	5	17	57,000
	No Rating	525,000	11	11	47,727
Total:		7,417,189	86	15	86,246
1982	BBB/Ba	60,000	2	11	30,000
	BB	1,378,000	16	12	86,125
	B	1,122,292	24	14	46,762
	CCC	145,050	2	13	72,525
	No Rating	92,311	4	23	23,078
Total:		2,797,653	48	14	58,284

1981	BBB/Ba	290,000	4	11	72,500
	BB	290,000	6	19	48,333
	B	893,667	15	18	59,578
	CCC	—	—	—	—
	No Rating	174,500	7	11	24,929
Total:		1,648,167	32	16	51,505
1980	BBB/Ba	50,000	1	7	50,000
	BB	418,000	9	18	46,444
	B	878,625	28	19	31,379
	CCC	25,000	1	15	25,000
	No Rating	70,000	4	14	17,500
Total:		1,441,625	43	18	33,526
1979	BBB/Ba	—	—	—	—
	BB	359,000	8	18	44,875
	B	852,600	33	18	25,836
	CCC	91,400	3	15	30,467
	No Rating	4,000	1	15	4,000
Total:		1,307,000	45	18	29,044
1978	BBB/Ba	40,000	1	20	40,000
	BB	407,875	10	19	40,787
	B	1,029,025	39	19	26,385
	CCC	12,000	1	15	12,000
	No Rating	4,000	1	15	4,000
Total:		1,492,900	52	19	28,710
Totals 1978 to 1985:		$45,726,927	618	14	$ 73,992

Source: Morgan Stanley & Co., Incorporated.

[a] Does not include convertibles, secondary offerings, exchange or best efforts offerings.

[b] BBB included if Moody's ranked below investment grade.

Table 2-6. Yield and Duration Comparison on Fixed Income Portfolios[a]

Portfolio		1978	1979	1980	1981	1982	1983	Average
High Yield Composite								
	Yield(%):	10.71	11.52	16.16	15.90	18.62	13.77	14.45
	Duration (years):	7.87	7.52	6.25	6.12	5.63	6.45	6.64
	Number of bonds:	153	203	243	280	286	339	
Shearson Lehman Long-Term Government Bond Index								
	Yield (%):	8.38	9.13	12.48	12.77	13.70	10.85	11.22
	Duration (years):	9.90	9.55	8.04	7.84	7.44	8.44	8.53
Portfolio by S&P Rating								
BB Rated Portfolio								
	Yield (%):	9.80	10.85	14.99	15.12	17.21	13.07	13.51
	Duration (years):	8.70	7.77	6.57	6.62	5.87	6.39	6.99
	Number of bonds:	34	51	61	49	55	70	
B Rated Portfolio								
	Yield (%):	10.83	11.79	16.73	15.96	18.50	14.20	14.67
	Duration (years):	7.84	7.67	6.23	6.17	5.57	6.27	6.63
	Number of bonds:	60	93	114	137	143	150	
CCC Rated Portfolio								
	Yield (%):	12.86	13.38	17.89	17.91	22.70	15.60	16.72
	Duration (years):	7.16	6.87	5.83	5.63	4.80	5.82	6.02
	Number of bonds:	17	14	16	33	21	35	

[a] Yields and duration are from 3/31 of each year and are weighted by the amounts outstanding.

amounted to $14.67 billion, slightly below 1984's total. This latter amount does not include exchange debt offers (discussed later), secondary issues which essentially represent existing debt repackaged and resold (over $1 billion in 1985) and any additional debt used to retire existing debt) that is not already included in exchange offers. The net total issued in 1985 was therefore 14.5% of the slightly greater than $100 billion of total corporate straight debt issued in 1985. There were 60 new issues greater than $100 million and 19 equal to or greater than $200 million (23 if we include exchange issues—Table 2-4b).

Table 2-5 indicates that while the 1985 total is slightly below the net 1984 total, a much larger number of issues were brought to the market (188). Therefore, the average issue size decreased from $120.6 million to $78.0 million. The breakdown of new issues by different bond ratings remained heavily skewed toward the B-rating, but a much larger proportion was nonrated; 41% of the new issues in 1985 were B-rated as compared to 55% in 1984 and 53% in 1983. The number of nonrated issues in 1985 soared to 63 of the 188 issues (33.5%) compared to just 15% in 1984 and 13% in 1983. The percent of CCC ratings remained fairly constant at 7.5% in 1985. Therefore, the proportion of issues rated B or below, including nonrated issues, was relatively high at 82% in 1985 compared to 77% in 1984 and 72% in 1983. This may indicate a deterioration in new issue credit quality in 1985—a point we will return to in Chapter 6. However, nonrated debt does not necessarily mean very low rated debt.

1986: PROSPECTS FOR A NEW RECORD YEAR

While 1985 came very close to being a record year for high yield debt new issues, 1986 will more than likely break all records. Already, all new issues through April 30, 1986 have totaled $13.8 billion, including $3.5 billion of nonrated bonds (Table 2-7). Since retirements were relatively small, under $1 billion, the supply of new high yield debt swelled the market considerably. There were 102 new issues in the first four months of 1986, including 38 nonrated and 39 rated B. The total rated high yield market was over $84 billion.

FALLEN ANGELS VERSUS ORIGINAL ISSUE HIGH YIELD DEBT

A frequent question posed by investors and analysts of the high yield debt market regards the proportion of that market comprised of debt that was originally issued as investment grade securities, "angels," but have since "fallen" from the graces of the investment community to low-grade or junk status. An investigation of this question as of December 1985 revealed the following statistics: Fallen angels accounted

Table 2-7. Total High Yield Bond Market: April 1986 (Including Exchange Issues)

	Amount ($MM)	Number of Issues	Number of Issuers
December 1985	$73,993	1,166	486
New issues (Rated January–April '86)	+10,290	+64	+50
Downgrades (January–April 1986)	+5,508	+27	+8
Upgrades (January–April 1986)	−4,672	−104	−7
Retired (January–April 1986)	−867	−18	−14
April 1986	$84,252	1,135	523

Source: Moody's Bond Record, monthly 1986, Standard & Poor's Bond Guide, monthly 1986, and Morgan Stanley & Co., Incorporated compilation.

for slightly over $23.2 billion of the $74.5 billion of rated debt, including exchange offers. Therefore, roughly 31% of the dollar amount of rated debt were fallen angels (Table 2-8). This proportion was up from the 29% total in June 1985 when $17 billion of fallen angel debt existed.

Of the $23 billion in December, approximately $8.8 billion (38%) were issued by public utilities and the remaining (62%) were issued by industrial and financial companies. The July 1985 proportion of public utility, fallen angels was substantially higher at 60% ($10.2 billion of the $17 billion outstanding). Thus, the recent trend appears to be a slight increase in the fallen angel proportion of high yield debt, but a dramatic change away from utilities and toward industrial firms. This trend continued in early 1986.

The number of fallen angel issues in December 1985 was 350, just under 30% of the total high yield bond issues outstanding. Of that number, 196 (56%) were public utility issues. Finally, only 65 of the 436 high yield issuers (15% were fallen angel companies. Therefore, a relatively small number of companies comprised the fallen-angel high yield debt segment, but a much larger percentage of the dollars and issues were from this category.

The fallen angel phenomenon was dramatically illustrated when on February 24, 1986 Phillips Petroleum's senior notes and debentures were downgraded by Moody's from Baa3 (the lowest investment grade rating) to Ba1 (the highest speculative or high yield rating). In recent years no other investment grade company had suffered such a precipitous drop in its credit rating quality; as recently as October 1982, its senior debt still carried the top-ranked triple-A rating. To be sure, Phillips' suffered enormously from the drop in oil prices in the mid-1980s and from a "successful" but costly defense against a hostile takeover battle which added unwanted debt to its financial structure in 1985.

Table 2-8. Fallen Angel (FA) Proportion of the High Yield Debt (HYD) Market

Fallen Angel Totals	June 1985	December 1985
Rated issues: Dollar amount ($MM)	$17,057	$23,164
Number of issues	351	350
Number of issuers	70	72
Utilities: Dollar amount ($MM)	$10,165	$8,758
Number of issues	228	196
Number of issuers	17	13
Total FA dollars / Total HYD outstanding	$17,057 / $59,078 = 28.9%	$23,164 / $74,514 = 31.1%
Total number of FA issues / Total HYD issues outstanding	351 / 1,070 = 32.8%	350 / 1,170 = 29.9%
Total number of FA issuers / Total HYD issuers outstanding	70 / 436 = 16.1%	72 / 488 = 14.8%

The debt of very large firms whose debt rating has dropped to the junk category in late 1985 and early 1986 has swollen the fallen angel proportion of the high yield debt market. For example, corporate mainstays such as Union Carbide, Texaco, Beatrice, and Phillips Petroleum have toppled to high yield status.

In the first four months of 1986, $5.5 billion of straight debt fell from investment grade to the low-rated (below Baa3 or BBB-) category, comprising 27 issues and 9 firms. Phillips Petroleum "contributed" the bulk of this debt with over $4.3 billion in downgraded issues. Over 100 issues involving $4.7 billion were raised to investment grade in this period. The vast majority came from upgraded electric utility issues, leaving only $5.7 billion or 6.7% of the high yield bond market in public utilities. Therefore, the net increase in the high yield market resulting from fallen angels was $837 million bringing the total dollar amount of fallen angels to $24 billion as of April 30, 1986. This represented 28.5% of the high yield debt market, since total rated debt was $84.3 billion (Table 2-7).

This recent development of an increase in nonutility fallen angel debt presents new opportunities to investors who remain confident about the eventual fate of these corporate giants. Still, size is no longer a proxy for financial health and the investor is cautioned to apply the same rigorous credit standards to multibillion dollar firms as he or she would to smaller, speculative companies. The recent (July 1986) default of the giant steel manufacturer, LTV Corp., with over $2 billion in public debt, is a graphic example.

EXCHANGE DEBT

An old financial restructuring strategy known as exchange debt offers has been utilized of late as never before. In 1985,

27 issues totaling $2.73 billion of exchange debt was issued to restructure balance sheets, primarily to avoid either bankruptcy or hostile takeovers (Table 2-9). This compares with just $702 million of distressed company exchange debt issued in 1984 (10 issues) and $486 million in 1983 (16 issues). Some of the larger recent distress exchange offers designed to avoid default/bankruptcy are listed in Table 2-10.

In a typical distress situation, exchange offers involve the option to swap existing high yield debt for a package of new securities which includes both new debt and an equity component. Acceptance of the offer must involve at least 85% of bondholders and is oftentimes accepted just before or even after the interest payment on the old debt is missed. Firms have a 30 day grace period after the official interest payment date to either pay the interest or work out an exchange.

Wahl and Fridson (1985) estimate that the average ex-

Table 2-9. High Yield Exchange Debt Issues: 1978 to 1985

Year	Number of Issues	Dollar Amount ($MM)	Average Amount ($MM)
1985	27	$2,725	$101
1984	10	702	70
1983	16	486	30
1982	5	529	106
1981	2	323	161
1980	5	646	129
1979	6	227	38
1978	12	662	55

Source: Morgan Stanley data base. Drexel Burnham Lambert's *High Yield Newsletter*, February 1986, lists only 12 successful exchange offers in 1985, although a number of these offers involved several issues each.

Table 2-10. Recent Distress Exchange Issues: 1985[a]

Company	Total Assets 1984 ($MM)	Par Amount Exchanged ($MM)	Financial Advisor (exchange)[c]	Exchange Expiration Date
LTV[b]	$6,926.0	$ 640.0	DBL/Lehman	9/23/85
Texas International	296.1	205.6	DBL	8/9/85
Petro-Lewis	947.8	197.0	DBL/PWMH	5/22/85
Petro-Lewis	947.8	190.3	DBL	12/23/85
Crystal Oil	459.8	333.0	PWMH	8/30/85
Lear Petroleum	710.3	180.0	DBL	11/6/85
American Quasar	163.8	95.0	DBL	7/19/85
U.S. Home Corp.	815.8	75.3	DBL	10/30/85
Beker Industries[b]	341.0	65.0	DBL	9/4/85
Western Company of N.A.	1,180.5	64.0	DBL	10/15/85
Tipperary	134.7	34.1	DBL	5/23/85
Rooney Pace	75.7	25.0	No Advisor	8/28/85
Texfi Industries	58.8	19.8	DBL	9/10/85
Quanex	282.3	15.0	DBL	5/23/85
Electro Audio Dynamics	39.6	7.7	DBL	3/15/85
		$2,147.0		

Source: Morgan Stanley compilation, F. Wahl, 1986 (not published).
[a] Firm has option to pay interest in common stock.
[b] Filed Chapter 11.
[c] DBL is Drexel Burnham Lambert; PWMH is Paine Webber Mitchell Hutchins.

change offer takes three months for successful completion which indicates that the process starts, in most cases, prior to the interest due date. They also discuss the purchase of exchange securities as an investment alternative.

In addition to bankruptcy avoidance, exchange debt benefits the ailing company by (1) reducing cash flow obligations, (2) reducing the nominal value of outstanding debt, (3) improving leverage and retained earnings ratios, and in some cases, (4) improving reported earnings.

Although a firm in distress will still suffer indirect bankruptcy costs due to the high probability of default, direct out-of-pocket bankruptcy costs will probably be lower than those incurred in Chapter 11 reorganization. The direct costs of bankruptcy include payments for bankruptcy administration, lawyers and accounting fees, expert witness fees, and so on (see Altman, 1984). It is true, however, that even in a debt restructuring, certain direct costs will be incurred including legal costs, investment advisory and underwriting fees, and the exchange premium that is usually offered to provide an inducement for debtholders to accept the exchange. We have not measured these fees but we presume they will be less than the combined direct and additional indirect costs of a Chapter 11 filing.

Since there is a serious stigma attached to the original issue's underwriter if that issue defaults, investment bankers will go to great lengths and costs to avoid legal defaults. At least one investment bank, Drexel Burnham Lambert, Inc., has organized an entire department, based in San Francisco and New York, with numerous "doctor-bankers" to attempt these workouts.

Exchange offers are not always accepted or may simply come too late to save the firm from eventual bankruptcy. To the extent that exchange offers are successfully accepted prior to the interest payment due date and the issue's rating is not downgraded to D, our default rate total (discussed later in Chapter 5), will be lower in the year of exchange acceptance. Some skeptics of high yield debt argue that a combination of debt restructuring and the large increase in new high yield debt in 1984 and 1985 leads to the conclusion that default rates in the future will increase—perhaps dramatically. We agree that future recession years will likely see relatively high *dollar* default levels. Keep in mind, however, that default rates are based on both the dollar amounts of defaults and the total population of outstanding high yield debt. If both the default numerator and population denominator grow, the default rate should remain somewhat stable, at least in normal economic growth years.

3

New Issuer Characteristics and Underwritings

NEW ISSUE HIGH YIELD DEBT

The concept of an original-issue high yield bond is relatively new, beginning in the late 1970s. Prior to this time, fallen angels made up the bulk of the market. The three year period of 1983 to 1985 was an explosive one for growth in high yield debt issues. Corporations began to accept and actively shift toward increasingly leveraged capital structures as a financial (and potentially defensive) strategy, due in part to the threat of hostile takeovers and the renewed concept of shareholder value maximization. Lowering interest rates motivated a great deal of original issues and refinancings in this period. Low rated and nonrated companies issued debt in order to finance internal growth, acquire others, do leveraged buyouts, repurchase shares, and so on.

The high yield debt market played and will continue to play a major role in supporting the emerging growth company movement in the United States. Since the vast majority of firms are not "investment grade" quality—at least in terms of their actual or prospective bond ratings—the opportunity for these firms to tap the public market has been an important development in accelerating their growth. Investment banks serving this field have also reaped substantial benefits from underwriting fees and subsequent trading profits.

In this section, we look at how the operating and financial profiles of new issuers have changed and the kinds of fees (underwriting gross spreads) the banks are receiving for placing or selling these bonds. With the increased competition for underwriting business going on today, one might expect a decrease in both the quality of issuer (at the margin) and underwriting fees. Unfortunately, 1985 saw the former, but not the latter. The following are some summary statistics for the years 1983 to 1985, when 398 new straight debt issues involving 321 firms came to market.

THE TYPICAL NEW HIGH YIELD BOND ISSUER

Table 3-1 summarizes the characteristics of new straight debt issues in 1985 and the comparable figures for 1983 to 1985 and 1978 to 1979. In 1985, the *average* new issue was just under $80 million in size although the *median* was lower at $60 million. There were at least 210 new issues, including exchange debt offers, with 188 of the straight debt variety. While the average bond rating in 1985 was slightly lower than in 1984, the *average* return on assets went up to 2.8% from 1.9% in 1984. The median return on assets also rose from 2.7% in 1984 to 3.5% in 1985. Despite this higher average return, the overall credit quality of new 1985 issues

Table 3-1. Profile of New High Yield Straight Debt Issues and Issuers: 1978 to 1985

	Average					Median					Standard Deviation				
	1978	1979	1983	1984	1985	1978	1979	1983	1984	1985	1978	1979	1983	1984	1985
Issue Characteristics															
Size of issue ($MM)	28.7	29.0	86.2	120.6	78.0	25.0	20.0	60.0	77.5	60.0	19.6	21.3	123.7	150.6	150.6
Coupon rate (percent)	—	12.3	12.0	13.3	12.9	—	12.3	11.8	14.5	13.9	1.0	1.1	1.8	3.9	3.4
Yield to maturity (percent)	—	12.6	14.0	15.2	14.9	—	12.6	13.8	15.4	14.7	1.1	1.2	1.3	1.4	1.3
S&P rating	B/B+	B/B+	B/B+	B/B+	B/B+	B/B+	B/B+	B/B+	B/B+	B/B+	—	—	—	—	—
Number of issues	52	41	86	124	188										
Firm Characteristics															
Age of firm (years)	22.8	26.0	28.2	31.1	36.0	18.0	20.0	20.1	26.0	26.0	14.7	19.6	22.4	23.1	30.5
Asset size ($MM)	176	285	1,074	1,588	1,108	107	127	322	735	410	187	487	1,776	2,435	2,154
Return on assets (percent)	—	—	1.5	1.9	2.8	—	—	2.7	2.7	3.5	—	—	7.8	8.2	9.8
Zeta score (issues)	−0.89	−0.76	−0.16	0.74	—	−1.15	−0.84	−0.30	0.78	—	1.7	1.3	3.4	3.3	—
Zeta score (firms)	−0.96	−0.54	−0.30	0.31	−0.86	−1.05	−0.84	−0.03	0.35	−0.24	1.5	1.2	3.0	3.1	3.0
Number of firms	50	40	68	99	135										

actually appears to have gone down. Our primary measure of overall quality is the Zeta™ score noted at the bottom of Table 3-1. In Chapter 6, we will discuss the Zeta technique and the overall credit quality trend concept.

The typical (median) new issuer in 1985 was 26 years old with $410 million in assets. The $60 million median issue size was equal to 1983's median but below the record year of 1984 when the median size was $77.5 million. The expected yield to maturity was 14.7% with a 13.9% coupon rate. The average coupon rate was lower than the median due to the number of discount and zero coupon bonds issued and falling interest rates.

Tables 3-2, 3-3, and 3-4 detail the frequency distributions found in Table 3-1 regarding the age, issue size, and assets of the firms studied. The distributions show the following:

- In 1985, 24% of the firms were relatively young (less than 15 years in business) while another 25% were in business for 15 to 24 years (Table 3-2). A rather large proportion (over 51%) of 1984 and 1985 new issuers were seasoned firms, in business over 25 years. This compares to 43% for 1978 to 1979 new issuers and 41% in 1983. The difference might be the result of more aggressive underwriting efforts and buyouts, as well as the robustness of the market. Surprisingly, the median age of new issuers 1983 to 1985 is only slightly above the 1978 to 1979 median (24 vs. 19).

- Table 3-3 lists the distribution by size of issue. The very small issue, under $20 million, proportion dropped again in 1985 to less than 4% but the moderate size categories ($21 to $60 million) increased to about 50% of all new

Table 3-2.   Age of Firm Distribution[a] (1983 to 1985 New Issuers)

Age of Issuer (years)	Number of Firms			Percent of Firms		
	1983	1984	1985	1983	1984	1985
0–4	8	11	7	10.4%	10.2%	6.3%
5–14	23	17	20	29.9	15.7	17.9
15–24	15	24	28	19.4	22.2	25.0
25–34	5	21	9	6.5	19.4	8.0
35–44	4	5	14	5.2	4.6	12.5
45–54	5	4	9	6.5	3.7	8.0
55–64	11	14	9	14.3	13.0	8.0
65–74	5	8	7	6.5	7.4	6.3
>75	11	4	9	1.3	3.7	3.0
Total sample	77	108	112	100.0	100.0	100.0
Average (yrs)	28	31	35	—	—	—
Median (yrs)	20	26	26	—	—	—

[a] Includes exchange debt issuers. Data not available on all firms.

Table 3-3.   Issue Size Distribution (1983 to 1985 New Issuers)

Size of Issue ($MM)	Number of Issues			Percent of Total Issues		
	1983	1984	1985	1983	1984	1985
0–20	7	6	7	8.1%	4.8%	3.7%
21–40	25	27	57	29.1	21.8	30.3
41–60	12	18	41	13.9	14.5	21.8
61–80	15	13	18	17.4	10.6	9.6
81–100	10	19	20	11.6	15.3	10.6
101–150	10	15	21	11.6	12.1	11.2
151–200	1	14	8	1.2	11.3	4.3
201–300	4	3	12	4.7	2.4	6.4
301–500	1	5	2	1.2	4.0	1.1
501–1000	—	3	1	0	2.4	0.5
> 1001	1	1	1	1.2	0.8	0.5
Total sample	86	124	188	100.0	100.0	100.0
Average size	$86.2	$120.6	$77.0	—	—	
Median size	$60.0	$ 77.5	$60.0	—	—	

Table 3-4.   Size of Firm (Total Assets) Distribution (1983 to 1985 New Issuers)

Size of Firm's Assets ($MM)	Number of Firms			Percent of Firms		
	1983	1984	1985	1983	1984	1985
0–100	14	12	24	20.3%	14.6%	21.6%
101–200	14	12	10	20.3	14.6	9.0
201–300	7	10	12	10.2	12.2	10.8
301–400	7	9	7	10.2	11.0	6.3
401–500	4	3	10	5.8	3.7	9.0
501–600	2	0	7	2.9	0.0	6.3
601–700	0	2	5	0.0	2.4	4.5
701–800	2	2	5	2.9	2.4	4.5
801–900	2	2	2	2.9	2.4	1.8
901–1000	2	1	3	2.9	1.2	2.7
1001–2000	5	12	12	7.2	14.6	10.8
2001–3000	6	6	1	8.7	7.3	0.9
3001–4000	0	1	6	0.0	1.2	5.4
4001–5000	1	4	1	1.4	4.9	0.9
5001–10000	3	5	5	4.3	6.2	4.5
> 10001	0	1	1	0.0	1.2	0.9
Total sample	69	82	111	100.0	100.0	100.0
Average size	$1,075	$1,588	$1,108	—	—	—
Median size	322	735	415	—	—	—

issues versus 36% in 1984 and 44% in 1983. Larger issues dropped back to 1983 levels.

- Firm size was impressive with over 23% (1985), 26% (1984), and 21% (1983) of the firms having assets over $1 billion (Table 3-4). Median total assets of new issuers in 1983 to 1985 was, as expected, considerably higher than the earlier 1978 to 1979 medians. No longer is the new issue market the primary province of the small, unseasoned company. Takeover issues had a very small impact on these statistics since there were relatively few issues of this type.

UNDERWRITERS

Drexel Burnham Lambert has been the leading underwriter (and driving force) in the high yield market for a number of years. Through 1985, that firm has been responsible for at least 287 issues and about 57% of the almost 46 billion new issue dollars since 1978. Drexel, once a relatively small firm in its field, became the second largest corporate bond underwriter in the United States securities industry in 1984 (according to *Securities Data Corp.*) behind Salomon Brothers, primarily because of its specialization in this new, high yield debt area. Table 3-5 and Exhibit 3-1 provide details on new issues and ratings by the underwriter.

In 1985, and even more so in 1986, Drexel Burnham Lambert faced more competition from a host of other investment banks. What was once an area to be eschewed by prestigious bankers, is now perceived by many banks as a high profit, almost glamorous area. Indeed, underwriting fees have averaged about 3% of new issue dollars and trading and

Table 3-5. New High Yield Public Debt Issues: 1978 to 1985[a]

	1985		1984		1983	
Underwriter	Amount	Number	Amount	Number	Amount	Number
Drexel Burnham Lambert	7,238,515	83	10,358,000	67	4,346,151	46
Salomon Brothers	1,464,311	13	865,000	9	422,538	4
Morgan Stanley	1,050,000	13	319,000	5	80,000	1
Lehman/Loeb	707,653	8	718,000	8	230,000	1
Merrill Lynch	665,776	9	530,000	4	427,000	5
First Boston	640,000	9	390,000	5	325,000	3
Goldman Sachs	615,000	5	100,000	1	125,000	1
Bear, Stearns	456,100	7	360,000	4	380,000	5
Prudential-Bache	435,000	8	950,000	13	275,000	6
E.F. Hutton	230,000	2	145,000	3	190,000	2
Blyth Eastman/Paine W.	206,044	2	65,000	1	235,000	3
Others	804,025	29	151,969	4	381,500	9
Total	14,670,424	188	14,951,969	124	7,417,189	86

[a] Bonds rated BB, Ba or lower, and high yield non-rated bonds. Includes utilities, excludes convertibles and exchange offers.
[b] In cases of consolidation, credit goes to surviving firm.

commission profits from secondary market activities have added handsome returns to underwriters and market makers.

The two firms that appear to have made the largest gains in this market in 1984 and 1985 are Salomon Brothers and Morgan Stanley. In 1985, both were the lead underwriter in over $1 billion of new debt involving 13 issues each. Drexel Burnam Lambert's market share "dropped" to about 50% of the straight debt new issue market in 1985. Salomon Brothers and Morgan Stanley followed with shares of 10% and 7% respectively. Drexel Burnam Lambert's market share would have been substantially larger if all types of high yield debt issues were included (i.e., exchange, secondary, and best effort offerings, etc.).

In early 1986, Drexel Burnham Lambert was still the leading underwriter, but firms such as Merrill Lynch, First Boston, Salomon Brothers, Goldman Sachs, Kidder Peabody, Morgan Stanley and Shearson Lehman are capturing an increasing share of the market, especially in the nonrated sec-

Full Credit to Lead Manager ($000)[b]

1982		1981		1980		1979		1978	
Amount	Number	Amount	Number	Amount	Number	Amount	Number	Amount	Number
1,543,800	28	935,667	19	498,000	15	408,000	14	464,500	15
—	—	60,000	1	115,000	2	—	—	—	—
—	—	—	—	40,000	1	—	—	—	—
25,000	1	225,000	2	222,500	5	75,000	2	75,000	2
699,000	7	240,000	4	50,000	1	75,000	1	157,875	3
—	—	—	—	—	—	171,000	1	68,750	3
35,000	1	30,000	1	105,000	4	235,000	7	120,775	6
40,000	1	—	—	—	—	30,000	2	20,000	1
82,542	2	25,000	1	89,125	2	68,000	4	90,000	3
225,000	1	—	—	52,000	1	173,000	4	155,000	3
147,311	7	132,500	4	270,000	12	72,000	10	341,000	16
2,797,653	48	1,648,167	32	1,441,625	43	1,307,000	45	1,492,900	52

tor. We expect this reduced market share for the "industry" leader to continue as competition heats-up.

GROSS UNDERWRITING SPREAD TRENDS AND ESTIMATION

As noted previously, competition among underwriters to bring high yield issues to market has become intense in recent years. While the fees from such endeavors, called underwriting spreads, cannot compare to fees from mergers and acquisitions, they are still profitable and average far more than spreads on investment grade issues. Indeed, these spreads frequently run as high as 4 to 5% of the issue size and average around 3%.

Gross underwriting spreads remained constant over the last 8 years at about 3.0% with a rather small and constant standard deviation of about 1.0%. Spreads in 1984 ranged from under 1% for some split-rated (BBB/Ba) issues to 4.75%.

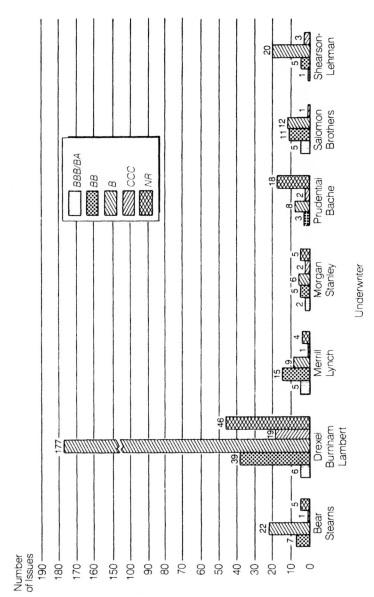

Exhibit 3-1 New high yield debt issues—underwriter by S&P bond rating 1978–1985.

Fifteen of 120 (12.5%) of the issues studied had gross spreads of 4.0% or greater in 1984 compared to 11 of 70 (16%) in 1983. In 1985, the range widened to between .45% and 7.5% with 33 'of the 174 issue sample (19%) being done at a cost of 4% or higher. This growth in the issues done at 4% or more may be a function of new underwriters getting into the market and issuing smaller, higher risk debt. We separated issues by size—$100 million or more and less than $100 million, and as expected, we found the average spread on larger issues underwritten between 1978 to 1985 to be some what lower (2.7% vs. 3.2% respectively) than the smaller sized deals. As the average deal size dropped in 1985, it is reasonable that average spreads would show marginal increases, which they did in most rating categories.

Underwriting gross spreads in this market continue to remain substantially above spreads for investment grade issues. The largest change occurred in the CCC and nonrated issues. Average spreads for these deals fell from the 4 to 6% range in 1979 to a low of about 3.0% in 1984. In 1985, they moved upwards again to the 3.3 to 3.7% levels, respectively. Table 3-6 and Exhibit 3-2 show the movement over time of the spreads of each rating category. Generally, while spreads have narrowed since 1978, they have held relatively stable in the 1983 to 1985 period [except CCC and nonrated (NR)], even though underwriting competition has heated up. These spreads, averaging three to five times those on A rated issues, make this market an attractive one to investment bankers.

Underwriting Spread Determinants

From an investment banking and issuer standpoint, it may be of some interest to examine the influences and possibly the determinants for gross underwriting spreads charged new issuers. Since the underwriting process is generally a

Table 3-6. Average Underwriting Gross Spreads for High Yield Issues (%)

S&P Rating	1978	1979	1980	1981	1982	1983	1984	1985	Average
A	0.74%	0.83%	0.72%	0.80%	0.80%	0.79%	0.71%	0.62%	0.73%
Number of issues:	122	63	102	72	70	124	106	193	
BBB/Ba	1.88%	—	1.90%	1.25%	1.63%	—	1.59%	1.29%	1.42%
Number of issues:	1	0	1	3	1	0	5	11	
BB	2.62%	2.33%	1.99%	2.38%	1.85%	2.04%	2.16%	2.21%	2.16%
Number of issues:	10	8	9	5	12	23	17	21	
B	3.29%	3.36%	3.27%	2.62%	2.30%	3.04%	2.91%	3.07%	3.04%
Number of issues:	38	33	24	11	21	44	52	71	
CCC	3.75%	4.68%	4.67%	—	3.65%	3.29%	3.21%	3.33%	3.48%
Number of issues:	1	2	1	0	2	3	7	12	
NR	5.5%	6.0%	6.0%	4.5%	3.69%	3.40%	3.32%	3.77%	3.76%
Number of issues:	1	1	2	3	4	11	16	59	
Average High Yield:	3.18%	3.29%	3.11%	2.64%	2.35%	2.81%	2.80%	3.11%	
Number of issues:	51	44	37	22	40	81	97	174	

Source: Morgan Stanley & Co., Incorporated, selected output.

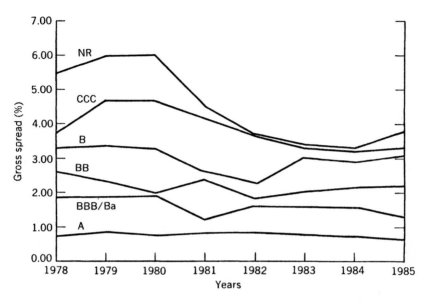

Exhibit 3-2 Underwriting gross spreads—for each S&P rating.

competitive one and there are many intangibles which impact pricing, the expected explanatory power of a quantitative model is uncertain. Still, there are certain conceptual and practical relationships which could lead to a meaningful and significant association. For example, the credit quality variables, that is, size, profitability, and solvency, should be negatively correlated with the selling effort and the charge by bankers to underwrite the issue. Also, since there are economies of scale in underwriting, we would expect a negative relationship between the size of the issue and gross spread. Since Zeta scores (our credit risk measure discussed in Chapter 6) captures many of the elements of credit quality, as does the S&P rating, we examined both.

In all, we examined the influence on spreads using seven potential determinants. These were age, size of issue, coupon rate, S&P rating, size of firm, return on assets, and credit quality (Zeta). Tables 3-7 and 3-8 list the primary variable correlations in 1983 and 1984 (1985 was not available). While there are numerous correlations of some significance, a few that stood out were gross spread (in 1983) which was highly correlated with (1) the S&P rating (positive), (2) the size of the issue (negative), (3) the size of firm (negative), and somewhat with (4) Zeta (negatively). We used these indicators as part of a regression estimate for gross spreads discussed in the following section. Zeta was highly correlated with the S&P rating (negative) and somewhat with the gross spread. Standard & Poor's ratings ranged from 1 (highest, BB +) to 10 (lowest, D).

Regression Results. We ran an ordinary, least squares regression of the relevant variables on gross spreads in 1983 and 1984 and then for the combined sample with the following specification and results:

$$GS = f \text{ (IS, TA, S\&P, Z)}$$

where GS = gross underwriting spread (in %)
    IS = issue size (in $ millions)
   TA = total assets (in $ millions)
  S&P = Standard & Poor's rating (BB+ = 1, BB = 2, etc.)
     Z = Zeta score from nearest statement date to issue

The results were:

For 1983

$$GS = 1.8860 - .00037(IS) - .00021(TA) + 0.2738(SP) - 0.01208(Z)$$
$$\quad\;\; (3.68) \qquad (-0.49) \qquad\quad (-2.69) \qquad\quad (2.93) \qquad\quad (-0.32)$$

t-statistics in parenthesis

$$R^2 = 59.6\%, N = 51$$

Table 3-7. New Issue Characteristics, High Yield Straight Debt-Correlation Matrix (1983 New Issues)[a]

	Age	Issue Size	Coupon	Gross Spread	S&P Rating	Total Assets	NP/TA	Zeta
Age	—							
Issue size	.053	—						
Coupon	.111	-.111	—					
Gross spread	-.203	-.311	-.133	—				
S&P rating	-.037	-.338	-.109	.630	—			
Total assets	.236	.220	.216	-.572	-.518	—		
NP/TA	-.317	.051	.148	-.045	-.203	-.003	—	
Zeta	-.213	.054	.136	-.280	-.522	.277	.283	—

[a] No Yield data available for 1983.

Table 3-8. New Issue Characteristics, High Yield Straight Debt-Correlation Matrix (1984 New Issues)

	Age	Issue Size	Coupon	Gross Spread	S&P Rating	Total Assets	NP/TA	Zeta	Yield
Age	—								
Issue size	.237	—							
Coupon	-.005	-.251	—						
Gross spread	-.176	-.252	.376	—					
S&P rating	-.130	-.252	.068	.557	—				
Total assets	.377	.615	.032	.346	-.437	—			
NP/TA	.008	.086	-.176	-.095	.083	.048	—		
Zeta	-.012	.225	-.420	-.360	-.277	.133	.579	—	
Yield	-.096	-.407	.412	.205	.310	-.309	-.086	-.248	—

Adj. R^2 = 55.5% (adjusted for d.f.)
DW = 2.08 (Durbin Watson test for autocorrelation)

For 1984

GS = 1.5529 − .00039(IS) − .00001(TA) + 0.2404(SP) − 0.0879(Z)
    (3.62)   (−0.48)   (−0.20)   (3.05)   (−.99)
    R^2 = 31.7% N = 58
    R^2 = 27.2% (adjusted for d.f.)
    DW = 1.38 (Durbin Watson test for autocorrelation)

Combined 1983 and 1984

GS = 1.6193 − 0.00016(IS) − 0.000044(TA) + 0.2640(SP) − 0.0691(Z)
    (5.22)   (−0.30)   (−0.89)   (4.63)   (−2.34)
    R^2 = 38.1%, N = 109
    R^2 = 34.5% (adjusted for d.f.)
  DW = 1.72 (Durbin Watson test for auto correlation)

The results for 1983 were far more significant with about 55 percent of the variation in gross spread explained. Less impressive were the results for 1984. The combined 1983 to 1984 regression indicates that about 35% of the variation in gross spread could be explained by our model.

Since the S&P rating is a very important variable and not always evident when pricing an issue, surrogates for the rating would have to be used if one wanted to predict spreads prior to issuance using this variable. We will observe (in Chapter 6) that the average Zeta scores for the different bond ratings were reasonable but apparently the variability is still large since the correlation of Zeta and S&P was −.522 and −.277 for 1983 and 1984, respectively. The correlation results in Tables 3-7 and 3-8 show Zeta's correlation with total assets at 0.277 and 0.133 in 1983 and 1984. Return on assets (NP/TA) registered 0.283 and 0.579 for 1983 and 1984, respectively.

These results are merely illustrative and since the explanatory power is not outstanding, we do not advocate utilizing such models directly in pricing. Still, we expect the correlations will prove useful to issuers and underwriters for understanding the high yield new issue market.

4

Investor Attractions: Mutual Funds and Other Investor Activities

HIGH YIELD DEBT AND THE INDIVIDUAL INVESTOR

The securities discussed in this book present classic risk-return tradeoffs which are embodied in the two names given to the market. High yield implies that the promised yield, and usually the coupon rate, offer premiums over other fixed income securities. Junk, on the other hand, implies higher risk than less speculative, investment grade debt. Are the risks worth it? What is the significance of higher coupon rates? How do we compare portfolios of different risk securities? All of these questions are posed and answered in the remaining chapters of this book.

As noted earlier, the relatively high risk on a number of individual high yield securities makes it difficult to operate in this market unless the investor can both diversify and assess the credit risk of the issuers in the portfolio. These "requirements" motivate our recommendation that professional investment managers should be used by individuals with limited analytical resources. For the average person, therefore, the primary vehicle should be open-end mutual funds. We will concentrate on these money managers in this chapter as well as noting other buy-side market participants. First, however, we will discuss the overall attractions to high yield debt securities.

HIGH YIELD ATTRACTIONS

The relatively high yields and superior annual returns in this market offer substantial potential benefits to investing institutions. One reason investors are drawn to this market is the power of yield premium compounding over time. Exhibit 4-1 shows the effects of a 300 and 500 BP difference in

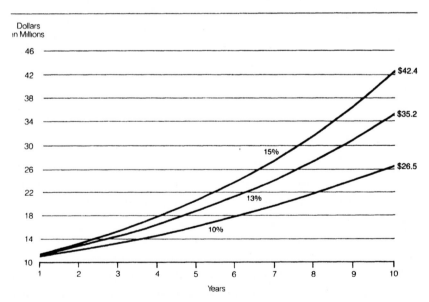

Exhibit 4-1   Effects of compounding over time $10 million starting value.

current yields between two bonds. After 10 years, a $10 million portfolio, invested (and compounded semiannually) at 10, 13, and 15%, would have resulted in final total holdings before taxes and charges of $26.5, $35.2, and $42.5 million respectively. A 300 BPs difference (13% vs. 10%) yields a 33% larger value at the end of 10 years. At the end of 20 years, the 300 BP advantage would have resulted in a 76% difference in the ending value. A 500 BP differential results in a 60% increase in wealth after 10 years, and so on. The longer the holding period, the greater the level of ending wealth, due to the impact of compounding. Compounding over time helps to lock in superior returns even after defaults and price fluctuations take their toll.

Table 4-1 illustrates, in more detail, this yield advantage over varying rates and time frames. For a number of "base rates" (rates on some less risky, benchmark security), the table shows the extra income that an investor will earn for various coupon rate (BP) premiums. For example, a 400 BP premium compared to a 10% base rate for 10 years will result in incremental returns of $1,217 from each $1,000 invested. The footnote to the table provides a step-by-step illustration. These impressive differentials assume that neither the benchmark nor the high yield securities default on interest or principal and the securities are held to maturity.

Table 4-2 illustrates a type of breakeven analysis showing the level of price deterioration a high yield investor can withstand without having his or her return fall below a comparable investment grade benchmark security. It explicitly considers the default possibility and provides an example of how the yield differential (spread) can protect against price deterioration due to default. To do so, it compares a high yield bond with a 12.5% coupon rate to an investment grade issue paying a 10% coupon rate. Hence, the current yield spread is just 2.5%, assuming both are selling at par value.

Table 4-1. Incremental Returns from $1,000 Invested and Reinvested at Various Yield Advantages Over Varying Lengths of Time[a]

Number of Years	Extra Income (Percentage Improvement)					
	5	10	15	20	25	50
8% Base Rate						
+200 BP (10%)	149 (10.1)	462 (21.1)	1,079 (33.3)	2,239 (46.6)	4,360 (61.3)	80,996 (160.4)
+300 BP (11%)	228 (15.4)	727 (33.8)	1,741 (53.7)	3,712 (77.3)	7,145 (104.6)	160,965 (318.7)
+400 BP (12%)	311 (21.0)	1,016 (46.4)	2,500 (77.1)	5,485 (114.2)	11,313 (159.2)	288,797 (571.8)
+500 BP (13%)	397 (26.8)	1,332 (60.8)	3,371 (103.9)	7,615 (158.6)	16,200 (227.9)	492,696 (975.5)
10% Base Rate						
+200 BP (12%)	162 (9.9)	554 (20.9)	1,421 (32.9)	3,246 (46.1)	6,953 (60.6)	207,801 (158.0)
+300 BP (13%)	248 (15.2)	870 (32.8)	2,292 (53.0)	5,376 (76.4)	11,840 (103.3)	411,700 (313.1)
+400 BP (14%)	338 (20.7)	1,217 (45.9)	3,290 (76.1)	7,934 (101.3)	17,990 (156.9)	736,215 (559.8)
+500 BP (15%)	432 (26.5)	1,595 (60.1)	4,433 (102.6)	11,004 (156.3)	25,723 (224.3)	1,251,579 (951.8)
12% Base Rate						
+200 BP (14%)	176 (9.8)	663 (20.7)	1,869 (37.5)	4,688 (45.6)	11,037 (59.9)	528,414 (155.7)
+300 BP (15%)	270 (15.1)	1,041 (32.5)	3,012 (52.4)	7,758 (75.4)	18,770 (101.9)	1,043,778 (307.6)
+400 BP (16%)	368 (20.5)	1,454 (45.3)	4,320 (75.2)	11,438 (111.2)	28,481 (154.6)	1,860,458 (548.3)
+500 BP (17%)	470 (26.2)	1,905 (59.4)	5,815 (101.3)	15,847 (154.1)	40,666 (220.8)	3,151,888 (928.9)

14% Base Rate

+200 BP (16%)	192 (9.8)	791 (20.4)	2,451 (32.2)	6,750 (45.1)	17,444 (59.2)	1,332,044 (153.5)
+300 BP (17%)	294 (14.9)	1,242 (32.1)	3,946 (51.8)	11,159 (74.5)	29,629 (100.6)	2,623,474 (302.3)
+400 BP (18%)	400 (20.3)	1,734 (44.8)	5,656 (74.3)	16,435 (109.8)	44,900 (152.4)	4,661,325 (537.2)
+500 BP (19%)	511 (31.9)	2,272 (58.7)	7,608 (99.9)	22,745 (151.9)	64,019 (217.3)	7,870,282 (907.0)

16% Base Rate

+200 BP (18%)	208 (9.6)	943 (20.2)	3,205 (31.8)	9,685 (44.6)	27,456 (58.5)	3,329,281 (151.3)
+300 BP (19%)	319 (14.8)	1,481 (31.8)	5,157 (51.2)	15,995 (73.6)	46,575 (99.3)	6,538,238 (297.2)
+400 BP (20%)	435 (20.1)	2,066 (44.3)	7,386 (73.4)	23,535 (108.3)	70,489 (150.3)	11,580,852 (526.5)

Source: The Case For High Yield Bonds, Drexel Burnham Lambert, Beverly Hills, CA, 1985.

[a] How to use: How much more can you accumulate by investing $1,000 at 15% rather than 12% over 15 years? Look under the 12% "Base Rate" case. Move across the "+300 BP" line (15%–12% = 300 BP) to the 15-year case. Answer: The extra 3% per year for 15 years will generate $3,012 of additional income, or 52.4% more income than the 12% investment. Note that as the base rate rises, incremental income increases. At a 16% base rate, the same 3% extra return per year generates $5,157 of additional income, vs. $3,012 of additional income, in the 12% base rate case.

Table 4-2. **Percentage of High Yield Principal Required to Maintain Return Equivalent to Investment Grade Bond**[a]

Year	Breakeven Price— % of Par Value
1	97.4
2	94.6
3	91.6
4	88.2
5	84.5
6	80.4
7	75.9
8	71.0
9	65.6
10	59.7
11	53.3
12	46.2
13	38.4

[a] Assumptions:
Yield spread on two bonds = 2.5% (10% vs 12.5%).
Interest payments reinvested at 9.5%.
Market interest rates remain constant.

The investment grade issue is assumed to be called at par value in the indicated breakeven year of the high yield bond's default. Intermediate cash flows (interest payments) are assumed to be reinvested in risk-free securities at a conservative 9.5%. The numbers indicate the price that the high yield bond must sell at (in the indicated year) for the investor to receive a return at least equal to the benchmark issue.

After 5 years, an investor in the high yield bond would have had to retain 84.5% of the bond's par value to have equaled the returns of an investment grade bond called at 100% of par in the same year. After 10 years, the price must be at least 59.7% of par and in year 13 the required price drops below 40%. The 38.4% level is actually below the 41% level we found to be the average market value of bonds just after default (see the default rate discussion in Chapter 5). This means that if a high yield portfolio experienced defaults of this magnitude at the end of the 13th year, then, on average, the portfolio would have performed as well as if funds had been invested in an investment grade portfolio.

If the current yield spread is greater than 2.5%, as was the case in recent years, then the number of years necessary to hold the high yield debt without default diminishes.

MAJOR INSTITUTIONAL INVESTORS

The high returns and the power of compounding have helped attract several types of major buy-side participants. These include mutual funds, pension funds, savings and loans, insurance companies, and a number of private trust and investment funds.

Mutual Fund Activities

At the end of 1984, there were 24 major funds that invested primarily in the high yield marketplace. At that time, Lipper Analytical Services, Inc. counted a total of 37 funds which held some level of high yield debt. A $10,000 investment split equally over each of the 24 major funds and invested for eight years from January 1, 1978 to December 31, 1985, assuming reinvestment of all dividend and capital gain payouts, would have resulted in a final portfolio worth $23,419. On an annual basis, this represents a bond equivalent return of 10.9%, substantially above the 5.6% return generated from long-term government bonds. Table 4-3

Table 4-3. Annual Returns (%) on Selected High Yield Funds[a]

Mutual Fund Name	1978	1979	1980	1981	1982	1983	1984	1985[b]
American Capital High Yield	—	2.2	1.4	5.8	30.2	16.4	8.7	25.1
American Investors Income Fund	3.0	15.1	18.4	−4.9	13.0	26.9	−8.4	22.7
CIGNA High Yield Fund	—	3.3	0.0	5.9	31.7	17.5	9.8	23.5
Colonial High Yield Securities	4.6	7.7	0.3	6.4	24.6	20.4	10.5	21.8
Dean Witter High Yield Securities	—	—	1.8	6.5	36.1	14.7	5.7	23.0
Delchester Bond fund	2.2	1.7	0.7	0.9	37.5	12.9	8.7	21.2
Eaton Vance High Yield Fund	0.4	−0.4	1.3	1.5	33.6	11.4	15.0	22.0
Federated High Income	1.0	6.6	2.7	3.9	32.5	14.5	10.8	21.7
Fidelity High Income Fund	3.8	4.6	4.4	6.9	35.8	18.5	10.5	25.5
First Investors Bond Appreciation	—	10.8	16.6	11.8	17.3	12.0	1.3	20.0
High Yield Securities	0.3	4.5	2.4	7.3	30.5	19.4	5.5	17.9
Kemper High Yield Fund	−4.9	2.4	−1.0	8.7	39.5	17.7	10.2	20.6
Keystone B-4 Bond Fund	4.2	1.6	8.3	10.0	31.5	15.4	4.9	19.9

Lord Abbett Bond Debenture Fund	2.9	7.0	8.9	5.3	27.5	16.6	5.0	21.0
Mass. Financial High Income Trust	—	6.8	5.3	7.3	35.8	26.7	6.4	23.1
Merrill Lynch Corp. Bond fund	—	2.4	3.1	6.5	23.1	18.4	8.6	21.6
Oppenheimer High Yield Fund	—	4.2	1.2	−6.3	28.8	14.7	3.5	18.8
Phoenix High Yield Fund Series	—	—	—	8.0	28.5	13.4	7.9	21.0
Prudential Bache High Yield Fund	—	—	4.9	4.0	28.1	15.7	10.2	20.6
Putnam High Yield Trust	—	2.8	7.0	5.2	38.9	15.6	7.0	19.9
Shearson High Yield Fund	—	—	—	5.1	32.2	14.8	9.8	18.8
United High Income Fund	—	—	7.8	5.3	32.7	13.9	9.6	23.3
Vanguard Fixed Income Securities	—	5.6	3.4	9.4	27.5	15.1	7.9	22.0
Venture Income (+)Plus	—	—	—	9.0	30.3	18.8	6.6	25.5
Average	1.8	4.9	4.7	5.4	30.3	16.7	7.3	21.8

Source: Wiesenberger Investment Company Service, division of Warren, Gorham & Lamont, Boston, Ma.
[a] Return: Change in value of initial $10,000 investment over one year period, reinvesting all income.
[b] Unaudited returns for 1985.

summarizes the returns for the 24 funds from 1978 to 1985. These results are from Wiesenberger Investment Company.

Lipper reported that when compared to various types of investment funds (United States Government, Corp. A Rated Bond, Corp. BBB Rated/Trading and General Bond), the high current yield bond funds outperformed the others, in terms of returns, in 6 out of the last 10 years (see Table 4-4). Only in 1984 were the high yield funds the worst performers. It has been suggested that the reason for the poor record in 1984 was that high yield mutual fund portfolios, had shorter durations and therefore underperform in a period of declining interest rates. The duration concept, mentioned in Chapter 2, will be returned to in Chapter 9.

As of December 31, 1985, the number of funds that Lipper classified as high current yield funds had swelled to 40 with $11.1 billion in net assets. By June 30, 1986 the amount invested by these funds (44 by then) increased to $20.2 billion.

A Survey. In order to further document the activities of high yield debt mutual funds we attempted to collect information from the 40 identifiable funds in existence in 1985. We received useful responses from 33 of them (listed in Table 4-5a). We were interested in the actual proportion of assets invested in high yield bonds, the degree of concentration within and across funds, particularly their dollar concentrations by issues, their holdings by industry sector and the popularity of individual issues with fund managers. These items, we felt, help to give the investor a better feel for the approach each of the funds is taking.

The 33 responding funds accounted for approximately 75% of the total assets under management by the 40 open-ended high yield funds in operation. The two largest funds in terms of market value were Putnam High Yield ($1.26 billion) and United High Income ($794 million), with the

Table 4-4. Returns on Selected Groups of Long Term Taxable Bond Funds: 1975 to 1985

	U.S. Gov't	Corp. Bond A Rated	Corp. Bond BBB/Trading	General Bond	High Current Yield Bond
1975	16.07%	15.91%[b]	18.03%	19.93%	23.94%[a]
1976	18.30	16.56[b]	21.39	24.27	29.82[a]
1977	0.31[b]	4.20	4.50	5.54	5.58[a]
1978	1.95	1.71	1.38	1.13[b]	2.21[a]
1979	4.39	1.40	−0.69[b]	0.11	5.57[a]
1980	5.72[a]	1.83	0.79	0.75[b]	4.68
1981	6.35[a]	4.59	4.31[b]	4.65	6.15
1982	23.59[b]	32.39	33.67[a]	33.28	29.40
1983	5.85[b]	7.97	9.08	10.06	16.77[a]
1984	12.43	12.77	13.70[a]	12.78	7.23[b]
1985	16.39[b]	20.99	23.15[a]	20.50	21.65
Ratio Best/Worst	2/4	0/2	3/2	0/2	6/1

Source: Lipper-Fixed Income fund Performance Analysis. Lipper Analytical Services, Inc. December 31, 1985. All income reinvested.
[a] Best compared to the other four strategies in a specific year.
[b] Worst compared to the other four strategies in a specific year.

Table 4-5a. High Yield Debt Mutual Fund Sample

Name of Fund	Date of Portfolio	Net Asset Value (Price per share)	Portfolio Turnover Rate (%)
AIM High Yield Securities	8/31/85	$ 9.91	66%
American Capital Group	8/31/85	10.21	82
American Investors Income	10/31/85	9.08	117
Bull & Bear High Yield	12/31/85	14.55	—
Bullock High Yield	12/31/84	10.78	50
Cigna High Yield	12/31/84	9.43	137
Colonial High Yield Securities	6/30/85	7.37	81
Dean Witter High Yield	12/31/85	13.40	126
Delchester Bond Fund	7/31/85	7.61	104
Federated High Yield Trust	11/30/85	10.63	—
Fidelity High Income	5/31/85	9.22	129
Financial Bond Shares	12/31/84	7.51	35
Franklin High Income	11/21/85	3.70	7
GIT	9/30/85	9.36	42
IDS Extra Income	8/31/85	4.92	89
Investment Trust of Boston HY Plus	11/1/85	14.58	26

J & W Seligman & Co.	11/18/85	7.59	—
Kemper High Yield	9/30/85	10.58	87
Keystone B-4 Bond Fund	7/31/85	7.92	43
Lord Abbett Bond Debenture Fund	9/30/85	10.37	—
Mass. Financial High Income	7/31/85	6.97	24
Merrill Lynch High Income	9/30/85	8.15	82
Oppenheimer High Yield	6/30/85	17.15	11
Pacific Horizon High Yield	8/31/85	15.49	263
Paine Webber High Yield	11/26/85	10.18	10
Pilgrim Group High Yield	10/31/84	7.98	36
Prudential-Bache High Yield	7/31/85	10.23	42
Putnam High Yield	11/22/85	15.40	160
Shearson High Yield	5/31/85	18.80	31
T. Rowe Price	11/30/85	10.52	6
United High Income	9/30/85	13.82	58
Vanguard Fixed Income High Yield	10/31/85	8.59	270
Venture Income Plus	11/29/85	11.17	165

Source: Information on each fund provided to the authors by the 33 funds.

average and median fund sizes being $250 million and $190 million respectively. As expected, most fund holdings were well diversified across a number of issuers. The vast majority held debt in at least 50 different firms, with the range running between 31 and 155.

Portfolio turnover rates (the dollar value of the shares bought or sold over the year relative to the funds total value), varied considerably, with the range extending from 6% (T. Rowe Price) to 270% (Vanguard). The unweighted average was 85%. Generally, the higher the turnover the more actively managed the fund is.

Table 4.5b lists practical investor information about the 33 high yield mutual funds in our survey. The minimum initial investment in such funds typically ranges between $250 and $1000, which makes them accessible to the small investor—even for individual retirement accounts (IRAs). About one-quarter are "no-load" funds but most funds do require a commission charge that can be over 8% of the offering price and over 9% of the net amount invested. Of the 33 funds, 10 are located in New York City and 6 in Boston. The rest are spread around the country with the majority located on the east coast.

Investment Policies of Mutual Funds. The overwhelming strategy of the high current yield mutual funds is to invest in debt securities rated BBB (Baa) or lower. The first impression of many observers is that high current yield means only low-grade or speculative issues. Lipper Analytical Services estimated recently, however, that only 70% of the net assets of the 40 high current yield mutual funds were invested in speculative issues (below triple-B). Our own investigation of prospectuses and from discussions with fund managers is that a not insignificant proportion of funds are invested in money market instruments and high quality debt issues.

In Table 4-6, we break down the funds' investments into corporate bonds, both high (HQ) and low quality (LQ), and all other investment securities. Note that there is a good deal of variation in the proportions between funds and also at different dates for the same fund. For example, the Kemper Fund invested 85.7% of their dollars in corporate bonds as of October 1985 and as much as 95% just four months later on February 1986. Although some of the funds invest virtually all of their dollars in high yield (low quality) debt, for example Seligman, Bull & Bear, High Yield Securities, Federated, T. Rowe Price, and Delchester, some others invest a large amount in investment grade securities. Out of the 33 mutual funds sampled, the percentage invested in high quality corporates varied from 0.0 to 24.0%. Therefore, average returns earned by the "so-called" high current yield group of funds will not conform exactly with the various high yield junk bond indexes available, including our own.

Fund Concentrations. In order to measure levels of dollar concentration by issuer, we ranked the securities of each fund by the amount invested in each company, selected the top 10 and 20% of the issuers and then compared the market value of these bonds relative to the fund's total market value (Table 4-7). This, while not a pure measure of concentration, helped to identify how a fund's value was distributed across the issuers it held. If one considers concentration levels to be another measure of diversification (albeit a rough surrogate only), we found Venture Income Plus and Dean Witter to be the most concentrated (and so least diversified) funds. Each had over 57% of its market value invested in the 20% of the issues in which it held the largest number of bonds. Both had over 33% invested in the top 10% of their share holdings. The Bull & Bear Fund and the Delchester Bond Fund, on the other hand, had the lowest concentration

Table 4-5b. Minimum Initial Investment, Sales Charge and Location for High Current Yield Mutual Funds

Mutual Fund Name	Minimum Initial Investment ($)	Maximum Sales Charge as Percent of Offering Price[c] (%)	Maximum Sales Charge as Percent of Net Amount Invested (%)	Telephone Number	City, State
AIM High Yield Securities	$1,250	6.50%($125,000)	6.95%	(713) 626-1919	Houston, TX
American Capital Group	500	6.75 ($25,000)	7.24	(713) 993-0500	Houston, TX
American Investors Income Fund[a]	400	0.00 —	0.00	(203) 622-1600	Greenwich, CT
Bull & Bear High Yield[a]	1,000	0.00 —	0.00	(212) 785-0900	New York, NY
Bullock High Income Shares	1,000	7.25 ($24,900)	7.82	(212) 513-4200	New York, NY
Cigna High Yield Fund	500	5.00 ($50,000)	5.26	(203) 726-6000	Philadelphia, PA
Colonial High Yield Securities Trust	250	4.75 ($25,000)	4.99	(617) 426-3750	Boston, MA
Dean Witter High Yield Securities	1,000	5.50 ($25,000)	5.82	(212) 938-4500	New York, NY
Delchester Bond Fund	25	8.50 ($10,000)	9.29	(215) 988-1241	Philadelphia, PA
Federated High Yield Trust	1,500	6.50 ($15,000)	6.95	(412) 288-1979	Pittsburgh, PA
Fidelity High Income[a]	2,500[d]	0.00 —	0.00	(800) 544-6666	Boston, MA
Financial Bond Shares[a]	1,000	0.00 —	0.00	(303) 779-1233	Denver, CO
Franklin AGE High Income	100	4.00 ($100,000)	4.17	(415) 570-3000	San Mateo, CA
GIT[a]	1,000	0.00 —	0.00	(703) 528-6500	Arlington, VA
IDS Extra Income Fund	2,000	5.00 ($50,000)	5.26	(612) 372-2897	Minneapolis, MN
Investment Trust of Boston HY Plus	1,000	6.75 ($50,000)	7.24	(617) 542-0213	Boston, MA
J & W Seligman & Co.	0	4.75 ($100,000)	4.99	(212) 488-0200	New York, NY
Kemper High Yield	1,000	5.50 ($100,000)	5.82	(312) 781-1121	Chicago, IL
Keystone B-4 Bond Fund[b]	250	4.00 —	4.17	(617) 338-3200	Boston, MA
Lord Abbett Bond Debenture Fund	1,000	8.50 ($10,000)	9.29	(212) 425-8720	New York, NY
Massachusetts Financial High Income	250	7.25 ($10,000)	7.82	(617) 423-3500	Boston, MA
Merrill Lynch High Income	1,000	4.00 ($50,000)	4.17	(212) 637-4300	New York, NY
Oppenheimer High Yield	1,000	6.75 ($25,000)	7.24	(212) 668-5055	New York, NY
Pacific Horizon High Yield Bond	1,000	0.00 —	0.00	(800) 645-3515	Newark, NJ

Paine Webber High Yield	1,000	4.25 ($25,000)	4.44	(212) 437-5326	New York, NY
Pilgrim High Yield	1,000	4.00 ($25,000)	4.17	(201) 461-7500	Fort Lee, NJ
Prudential-Bache High Yield[b]	1,000	5.00 —	5.26	(212) 791-3920	New York, NY
Putnam High Yield	500	6.75 ($25,000)	7.24	(617) 292-1000	Boston, MA
Shearson High Yield	500	3.75 ($25,000)	3.90	(212) 577-5794	New York, NY
T. Rowe Price High Yield[a]	1,000	0.00 —	0.00	(800) 638-5660	Baltimore, Md
United High Income	1,000	8.50 ($15,000)	9.29	(816) 283-4000	Kansas City, MO
Vanguard Fixed Income High Yield[a]	3,000	0.00 —	0.00	(215) 964-2600	Valley Forge, PA
Venture Income Plus	1,000	8.50 ($10,000)	9.29	(505) 983-4335	Santa Fe, NM

[a] No-load fund.
[b] Sales charge depends on length of investment period.
[c] Sales charge as percentage of offering price = sales charge/ (net asset value + sales charge); sales charge as percentage of net amount invested = sales charge/net asset value; amount of investment applicable to the maximum sales charge in parentheses. Reduction in percentage for larger investments.
[d] $250 for IRA accounts.

73

Table 4-6. Investment Policies of High Current Yield Mutual Funds: Proportion Invested by Types of Securities

Mutual Fund	Date	Source[a]	Corporate Bonds and Notes			Government Security	Cash, S-T Notes, Receivables	Stock and Warrants	Other Assets	Total
			Total	HQ[b]	LQ[c]					
Kemper High Yield	10/85	P	85.70	—	—	2.00	2.80	2.70	6.80	100.00
	2/86	T	95.00	10.00	90.00	—	5.00	—	—	100.00
Financial HY	3/85	P	78.48	—	—	—	17.33	4.19	—	100.00
	3/86	T	92.60	—	—	—	6.40	1.00	—	100.00
GIT Income Trust	9/85	P	88.40	—	—	0.2	—	—	11.40	100.00
	9/85	T	88.40	0.00	100.00	0.2	—	—	11.40	100.00
Seligman High Inc.	—	P	No information							
	3/86	T	100.00	0.00	100.00	—	—	—	—	100.00
Dean Witter HY	10/85	P	91.60	—	—	1.2	0.40	4.00	2.80	100.00
		T	97.00	6.00	94.00	—	—	3.00	—	100.00
Investment Trust of Boston HY Plus	—	P	No information							
	1/86	T	95.00	—	—	—	3.20	—	—	98.20
Putnam High Yield	11/85	P	89.53	—	—	3.26	5.32	2.99	—	101.10
	2/86	T	96.80	16.40	83.60	3.20	—	—	—	100.00

Prudential-Bache HY	7/85	P	91.00	—	—	—	5.40	1.80	1.80	100.00
	3/85	T	95.00	—	—	—	5.00	—	—	100.00
Merrill Lynch	9/85	P	93.30	—	—	—	1.30	0.50	4.90	100.00
	4/86	T	95.00	13.7[d]	86.30	—	5.00	—	—	100.00
Keystone B-4	9/85	P	81.30	—	—	15.00	2.80	0.90	—	100.00
	3/86	T	99.00	15.90	—	—	1.00	—	—	100.00
Oppenheimer HY	7/85	P	94.20	—	—	—	1.50	0.40	3.90	100.00
	—	T	Not Available							
CIGNA HY	1/86	P	98.90	0.00	100.00	—	—	1.10	—	100.00
	—	T	Not Available							
Vanguard	10/85	P	97.70	—	—	—	8.20	1.80	-7.70	100.00
	2/86	T	95.80	0.00	100.00	—	1.60	2.60	—	100.00
Bull & Bear HY	6/85	P	No information							
	4/86	T	100.00	0.00	100.00	—	—	—	—	100.00
Paine Webber HY	12/85	P	No information							
	3/86	T	98.50	0.00	100.00	—	1.50	—	—	100.00
Mass. Financial	7/85	P	82.00	—	—	1.90	7.80	8.30	—	100.00
High Inc.	1/86	T	95.00	0.00	100	—	2.00	3.00	—	100.00

[a] P = Prospectus; T = Telephone contact
[b] HQ—Bonds rated above BBB (investment grade)
[c] LQ—Bonds rated BBB and lower (medium→lower grade issues)
[d] High quality category also includes bonds rated BBB

Table 4-6. *(continued)*

Mutual Fund	Date	Source[a]	Corporate Bonds and Notes			Government Security	Cash, S-T Notes, Receivables	Stock and Warrants	Other Assets	Total
			Total	HQ[b]	LQ[c]					
Federated High Inc.	11/85	P	No information							
	3/86	T	99.00	0.00	100.00	—	1.00	—	—	100.00
Federated HY	11/85	P	No information							
	3/86	T	99.00	0.00	100.00	—	1.00	—	—	100.00
High Yield Sec.	1/86	P	89.93	—	—	—	4.97	3.25	—	98.15
	1/86	T	89.00	0.00	100.00	—	9.00	2.00	—	100.00
T. Rowe Price HY	11/85	P	99.10	—	—	4.60	0.10	—	−3.8	100.00
	11/85	T	99.10	1.00	99.00	4.60	0.10	—	−3.8	100.00
Venture Income Plus	—	P	No information							
	3/86	T	86.60	0.00	100.00	—	3.70	9.70	—	100.00
Franklin AGE H-Inc.	—	P	No information							
	4/86	T	93.00	0.00	100.00	—	7.00	—	—	100.00
Pacific Horizon	9/85	P	95.50	—	—	—	4.50	—	—	100.00
	4/86	T	91.90	—	—	—	8.10	—	—	100.00
Delchester Bond	7/85	P	96.89	—	—	0.68	2.43	—	—	100.00
	3/86	T	97.00	1.00	99.00	—	3.00	—	—	100.00

American Capital	1/86	P	No information							
	2/86	T	95.00	0.00	100.00	—	5.00	—	—	100.00
IDS Extra Inc.	10/85	P	88.30			6.90	0.50	2.00	—	97.70
	3/86	T	90.00	24.00	76.00	13.00	—	—	—	103.00
Shearson HY	7/85	P	86.10			0.90	8.70	0.20	4.1	100.00
	1/86	T	89.00	17.00	83.00	—	11.00	—	—	100.00
Bullock High Inc.	4/85	P	96.18			—	3.82	—	—	100.00
		T	Not available							
Colonial HY Sec.	6/85	P	92.00	5.70	—	—	1.00	0.10	6.9	100.00
	3/86	T	96.50	1.76	98.24	—	3.50	—	—	100.00
American Investors	10/85	P	95.19				—	2.23	2.58	100.00
		T	Not available							
Fidelity High Inc.	7/85	P	80.10			10.40	6.20	3.20	0.1	100.00
	1/86	T	78.40	0.00	100.00	8.10	13.20	0.20	0.1	100.00
United Funds Group		P	No information							
		T	Not available							
Lord Abbett Group	9/85	P	85.19	8.83	47.63	1.56	—	9.04	4.21	100.00
	9/85	T	85.19	8.83	47.63	1.56	—	9.04	4.21	100.00
Pilgrim High Yield	3/85	P	95.50					—	4.5	100.00
	12/85	T	93.90	0.00[d]	100.00	—	3.20	2.90	—	100.00

[a] P = Prospectus; T = Telephone contact
[b] HQ—Bonds rated above BBB (investment grade)
[c] LQ—Bonds rated BBB and lower (medium→lower grade issues)
[d] High quality category also includes bonds rated BBB

Table 4-7. High Yield Debt Mutual Fund Portfolio Concentration: Proportion Invested in Top 10% and 20% (by Market Value)

Name of Fund	Number of Companies in Portfolio	Total Market Value ($000 omitted)	Amount Invested in Top 10% to Total Market Value	Amount Invested in Top 20% to Total Market Value
AIM High Yield Securities	70	$ 79,488	23.03%	37.67%
American Capital Group	100	450,450	22.02	40.37
American Investors Income	43	20,427	17.65	30.21
Bull & Bear High Yield	37	31,489	13.45	23.38
Bullock High Yield	42	86,880	19.27	35.85
Cigna High Yield	56	140,428	16.45	28.70
Colonial High Yield Securities	78	96,496	17.72	31.23
Dean Witter High Yield	98	535,141	39.07	57.13
Delchester Bond Fund	56	56,942	14.90	25.98
Federated High Yield Trust	42	12,343	15.69	27.98
Fidelity High Income	155	450,524	30.07	51.72
Financial Bond Shares	31	3,191	16.36	32.45
Franklin High Income	63	229,862	22.99	39.78
GIT	52	8,746	18.66	32.61
IDS Extra Income Fund	116	475,587	16.07	28.32

Investment Trust of Boston HY Plus	110	19,047	19.30	33.74
J & W Seligman & Co.	38	29	17.46	34.93
Kemper High Yield	64	191,631	31.27	47.78
Keystone B-4 Bond Fund	147	553,940	20.69	35.17
Lord Abbett Bond Debenture Fund	87	233,633	16.91	32.58
Mass Financial High Income	144	382,008	31.38	45.76
Merrill Lynch High Income	79	279,169	18.76	33.08
Oppenheimer High Yield	112	433,142	29.94	49.20
Pacific Horizon High Yield	49	10,132	21.66	37.43
Paine Webber High Yield	71	114,013	18.13	30.96
Pilgrim Group High Yield	37	11,296	17.74	33.86
Prudential-Bache High Yield	116	277,469	23.25	37.00
Putnam High Yield	113	1,255,064	30.80	46.64
Shearson High Yield	118	189,530	24.04	37.52
T. Rowe Price	110	303,947	22.73	40.95
United High Income	155	793,999	29.32	39.04
Vanguard Fixed Income High Yield	121	482,962	18.83	33.97
Venture Income Plus	58	40,656	33.42	57.45
		Total $8,249,661	Average 22.09%	Average 37.29%

Source: Information on each fund provided to the authors by the 33 Funds.

levels with 23.4 and 26.0% invested in the top 20% of their issuers and 13.5 and 12.6% in the top 10%, respectively.

Does level of concentration or diversification mean better returns? Not necessarily. There are just too many factors that play a role in the return equation. However, it is interesting to note that both Venture Income Plus and Dean Witter were at or near the top of the rating ranking for 1985, while the two least concentrated funds produced very close to the average return, as might be expected (see Table 4-3).

Industry Breakdown. In terms of industry concentration, the largest sector's representation in high yield mutual funds was manufacturers, with about 36% of the total issues invested in. This is a slightly lower proportion than the available securities in the market (40%). Table 4-8 lists both the funds' investment by industry as well as the market proportions. Following manufacturers in popularity, we find entertainment, finance, oil and gas, and communication bonds next in percent representation—each with about 8 to 11% of the total. Note that fund managers tended to underinvest, on a relative basis, in finance companies (8.9% vs. 14.5% available) and manufacturing (35.9% vs. 40.5% available) and emphasized more the entertainment sector (11.1% vs. 8.3% available) and to a lesser extent many of the remaining sectors. However, in general, fund managers diversified more or less according to available industry sector representation.

Individual Company Popularity. The three most commonly found individual companies (not issues) were all public utilities with Consumers Power Co. and Middle South Energy represented in 24 of the 33 funds (Table 4-9). Long Island Lighting was just behind with 23 funds holding at least one of its issues. This may be a result of the extraordinarily large number of issues that public utilities have

Table 4-8. Portfolio Fund Investments in High Yield Debt by Industry (Number of Issues)[a]

Industry	Number of Issues in Each Industry	Percent by Industry (Total Invested by Mutual Funds)	Percent by Industry (Total Available Securities)
Manufacturing	204	35.9%	40.5%
Entertainment	42	11.1	8.3
Finance	73	8.9	14.5
Oil and gas	45	8.6	8.9
Communication	24	7.9	4.8
Medical	24	6.3	4.8
Utility	18	6.2	3.6
Retail	23	6.0	4.6
Airline	22	5.2	4.4
Transportation	18	2.8	3.6
Conglomerates	11	1.1	2.2
	504	100.0%	100.0%

Source: Portfolio breakdowns provided by individual funds to the authors.

[a] Each mutual fund's contribution is measured as of their last available portfolio release. Most funds are as of mid to late 1985 (see Table 4–5 for exact dates). Sample consists of 33 mutual funds.

81

Table 4-9. The Most Popular High Yield Debt Issuers Held by Mutual Funds[a]

Issuer	Industry	Number of Funds Holding Issuer	Percent of Total Funds (33)
Consumers Power Co.	Utility	24	72.7%
Middle South Energy	Utility	24	72.7
Long Island Lighting	Utility	23	69.7
Minstar	Manufacturing	20	60.6
International Harvester	Manufacturing	19	57.6
People Express	Airline	19	57.6
Harnischfeger	Manufacturing	17	51.5
Pantry Pride	Retail	17	51.5
Republic Health	Medical	17	51.5
Mattel	Entertainment	17	51.5
Wickes Companies	Retail	17	51.5
Texas Air Corp.	Airline	17	51.5
Swan Brewing	Manufacturing	16	48.5
MCI Communications	Communication	16	48.5
Resorts International Inc.	Entertainment	16	48.5
Turner Broadcasting System	Communication	16	48.5
MacAndrews & Forbes Group	Manufacturing	16	48.5
LTV Corp.	Manufacturing	16	48.5
Nortek	Manufacturing	16	48.5
I.C.H. Corp.	Finance	15	48.5
Price Communications	Communication	15	45.5
Jones Intercable	Entertainment	15	45.5
ACF Industries	Manufacturing	15	45.5
Conair Acquisition	Finance	15	45.5
United Cable Television	Communication	15	45.5

Coast Savings & Loan Assoc.	Finance	14	42.4
Triangle Industries	Manufacturing	14	42.4
Grolier Inc.	Entertainment	14	42.4
Eastern Air Lines	Airline	14	42.4
Nu-Med	Medical	14	42.4
Chicago & Northwestern Railway	Transportation	13	39.4
Coleco Industries	Manufacturing	13	39.4
Woodward & Lothrop	Retail	13	39.4
Gelco Corp.	Finance	13	39.4
Oak Industries	Communication	13	39.4
Petro-Lewis Corp.	Oil	13	39.4
Pan American World Airways	Airline	13	39.4
McLean Industries	Manufacturing	12	36.4
General Defense Corp.	Manufacturing	12	36.4
Public Service Co. of New Hampshire	Utility	12	36.4
Republic Airlines	Airline	12	36.4
United Merchants & Manufacturers	Manufacturing	12	36.4
Resorts International Financing	Entertainment	12	36.4
ARA Holdings	Finance	12	36.4
Crystal Oil	Oil	12	36.4
Republic Steel Corp.	Manufacturing	11	33.3
AMAX Inc.	Manufacturing	11	33.3
McCrory Corp.	Retail	11	33.3
Health Resources Corp. of America	Medical	11	33.3
Beverly Enterprises	Medical	11	33.3
Public Service Co. of Indiana	Utility	11	33.3
Global Marine	Oil	11	33.3
Arrow Electronics	Manufacturing	11	33.3
Metromedia	Communication	11	33.3

a Those held by over 33% of funds.

outstanding relative to other sectors. The leading manufacturers in terms of popularity were Minstar Corp. and the venerable International Harvester Corp. (now Navistar Inc.). The former issued a large, immensely popular offering in 1985. The latter's appearance is interesting because investors, in 1985, must have felt comfortable with the default likelihood of this company which only two years earlier was clearly on the brink of disaster.

For some managers, however, an investment in seemingly attractive Minstar turned sour when in May 1986 Minstar announced that it would invoke a little known clause in its bond indenture to begin calling in, at par value, 10% ($30 million worth) of the outstanding issue. The clause entitled Minstar to call in 10% of the issue each 6 months if the firm's "adjusted net worth" falls below $135 million (which it did). Intangible assets are deducted from net worth. Included in intangibles is the value of marketable securities which normally are not treated as such. A number of other recently issued junk bonds have the same clause and the risk of call was thought to be high in the wake of the Minstar call. Through the end of May 1986 over $4 billion worth of junk bond debt was called, mainly due to the falling level of interest rates in 1985 and 1986. The risk of call, while prevalent in all corporate debt risk classes, has caused some investors to become wary of junk bonds vis-à-vis available noncallable fixed income instruments.

The most popular airlines were People's Express (19) followed by Texas Air Corp. (17), Eastern Airlines (14), and Republic Airlines (12). Another popular company that is recovering from financial distress, indeed from a Chapter 11 bankruptcy reorganization, was Wickes with 17 funds holding its restructured debt. Several entertainment and communication companies were held by many funds. For example, Resorts International (16) and its financing subsidiary (12) were fairly popular. Overall, however, manufacturing issues were by far the most popular holdings of fund managers. Unfortunately, 16 of the 24 funds held at least one issue of the ill-fated LTV Corp., which filed for bankruptcy in July 1986. We do not know how many actually held LTV just prior to default.

Tables 4-10 through 4-20 list the most popular companies broken into their industrial categories including manufacturing, entertainment, finance, oil & gas, communication, medical, utility, retail, airlines, transport, medical, and conglomerates.

Table 4-10. The Most Popular Manufacturing High Yield Debt Issuers Held by Mutual Funds[a]

Issuer	Number of Funds Holding Issuer	Percent of Total Funds (33)
Minstar	20	60.6%
International Harvester	19	57.6
Harnischfeger	17	51.5
MacAndrews & Forbes Group	16	48.5
Swan Brewing	16	48.5
Nortek	16	48.5
LTV Corp.	16	48.5
ACF Industries	15	45.5
Triangle Industries	14	42.4
Coleco Industries	13	39.4
United Merchants & Mfrs.	12	36.4
General Defense Corp.	12	36.4
McLean Industries	12	36.4
AMAX Inc.	11	33.3
Republic Steel Corp.	11	33.3
Arrow Electronics	11	33.3
Standard Pacific	10	30.3
Danaher	10	30.3
Hyponex	9	27.3

Table 4-10. (*continued*)

Issuer	Number of Funds Holding Issuer	Percent of Total Funds (33)
United Brands	9	27.3
Bally's Health & Tennis	9	27.3
A.R.A. Mnfg. Co. of Delaware	8	24.2
Savin Corp.	8	24.2
Quanex Corp.	8	24.2
Radice Corp.	8	24.2
Beker Industries Corp.	8	24.2
Hovnanian Enterprises	8	24.2
CTI International Inc.	8	24.2
Intermark	8	24.2
Newport Steel	7	21.2
Athlone Industries	7	21.2
Walter (Jim)	7	21.2
Stone Container	7	21.2
American Sign & Indicator	7	21.2
Federal Paper Board	7	21.2
National Propane Corp.	7	21.2
Levi Strauss	7	21.2
Chris Craft Industries	7	21.2
Digicon Inc.	7	21.2
General Development	7	21.2
Western Pacific Industries	7	21.2

[a] Those held by over 20% of funds.

Table 4-11. Entertainment High Yield Debt issuers Held by Mutual Funds

Issuer	Number of Funds Holding Issuer	Percent of Total Funds
Mattel	17	51.5%
Resorts International Inc.	16	48.5
Jones Intercable	15	45.5

Issuer	Number of Funds Holding Issuer	Percent of Total Funds
Grolier Inc.	14	42.4
Resorts International Fin.	12	36.4
Plitt Theater Holdings	10	30.3
Six Flags	10	30.3
Elsinore Corp.	10	30.3
Cannon Group	9	27.3
Circus Circus Enterprises	9	27.3
Cablevision System Dev.	8	24.2
Bally's Park Place Funding	8	24.2
Golden Nugget Inc.	8	24.2
Thousand Trails	7	21.2
MGM Grand Hotels	7	21.2
Orion Pictures	6	18.2
Caesars World Fin.	5	15.2
Tri-Star Pictures	5	15.2
Plitt Theater	5	15.2
Showboat Inc.	5	15.2
Mickleberry Corp.	4	12.1
Shaughnessy Dev. Corp.	4	12.1
Vagabond Hotel	4	12.1
Caesars World Inc.	4	12.1
Golden Nugget Financial Corp.	4	12.1
Elsinore Finance Corp.	4	12.1
Lorimar Productions	3	9.1
Days Inn of America	3	9.1
New World Picture	3	9.1
Spendthrift Farms	3	9.1
Trump's Castle Funding	3	9.1
GNAC	2	6.1
Twentieth Century-Fox Film	2	6.1
MGM/UA Entertainment	1	3.0
Sahara Resorts	1	3.0
Horn & Hardart Co.	1	3.0
Ramada Inns	1	3.0
Pizza Time Theater	1	3.0

Table 4-11. (*continued*)

Issuer	Number of Funds Holding Issuer	Percent of Total Funds
Hacienda Resorts	1	3.0
Northview Corp.	1	3.0

Table 4-12. Finance High Yield Debt Issuers Held by Mutual Funds

Issuer	Number of Funds Holding Issuer	Percent of Total Funds
I.C.H. Corp.	15	45.5%
Coast Savings & Loan	14	42.4
Gelco Corp.	13	39.4
ARA Holding	12	36.4
American Continental	8	24.2
Washington Mutual	8	24.2
Guarantee Savings	7	21.2
Comdisco	7	21.2
Western Savings & Loan	7	21.2
Commonwealth Savings	6	18.2
Reliance Group Holdings	5	15.2
Southmark	5	15.2
Landmark Bancshares	4	12.1
Homestead Savings & Loan	4	12.1
International Banknote	4	12.1
Integrated Resources	4	12.1
Itel	3	9.1
Chrysler Financial	3	9.1
Leasco Corp.	3	9.1
Vis Capital Corp.	3	9.1
Realty Refund	3	9.1
Home Federal S&L Tucson	3	9.1
Far-West Saving & Loan	3	9.1
Reliance Group	3	9.1

Issuer	Number of Funds Holding Issuer	Percent of Total Funds
Financial Trust Co.	2	6.1
Maxxam Group	2	6.1
Foothill Group Inc.	2	6.1
Financial Corp. of America	2	6.1
Varco Intl. Finance N.V.	2	6.1

Table 4-13.   Oil & Gas High Yield Debt Issuers Held by Mutual Funds

Issuer	Number of Funds Holding Issuer	Percent of Total Funds
Petro-Lewis Corp.	13	39.4%
Crystal Oil	12	36.4
Global Marine	11	33.3
Forest Oil Corp.	10	30.3
Phillips Petroleum	10	30.3
Coastal Corp.	9	27.3
Valero Energy	9	27.3
Hudson's Bay Oil & Gas	8	24.2
Valero Natural Gas	8	24.2
Occidental Petroleum	8	24.2
Damson Oil Corp.	7	21.2
Argo Petroleum	6	18.2
Texas International Co.	6	18.2
American Quasar Petroleum	6	18.2
Tesoro Petroleum	6	18.2
Universal Resources	6	18.2
Lear Petroleum	5	15.2
Wainoco Oil Co.	4	12.1
Western Co. of North America	4	12.1
Triton Energy	4	12.1
Buttes Gas & Oil	3	9.1
Basix Corp.	3	9.1
Consolidated Oil & Gas Co.	3	9.1

Table 4-13. *(continued)*

Issuer	Number of Funds Holding Issuer	Percent of Total Funds
Mesa Petroleum	2	6.1
Moran Energy	2	6.1
Getty Petroleum	2	6.1
Internorth	2	6.1
Texas American Oil Corp.	2	6.1
Texaco Capital N.V.	1	3.0
Oxoco Inc.	1	3.0
Anglo Co.	1	3.0
Chapman Energy	1	3.0
Production Operators Corp.	1	3.0
Page Petroleum	1	3.0
Niantic Bay Fuel	1	3.0
Moran Brothers Inc.	1	3.0
LPC International Finance	1	3.0

Table 4-14. Communication High Yield Debt Issuers Companies Held by Mutual Funds

Issuer	Number of Funds Holding Issuer	Percent of Total Funds
Turner Broadcasting System	16	48.5%
MCI Communications	16	48.5
United Cable Television	15	45.5
Price Communications	15	45.5
Oak Industries	13	39.4
Metromedia	11	33.3
Canadian Cablesystems Ltd.	10	30.3
SFN Companies	10	30.3
Prime Cable of Georgia	10	30.3
Warner Communications	7	21.2
Harte-Hanks Comm./Cable	10	30.3
Blair (John) & Co.	7	21.2
Communications Corp. of Am.	4	12.1

Issuer	Number of Funds Holding Issuer	Percent of Total Funds
Western Union Corp.	3	9.1
Tele-Communications	3	9.1
Texscan Corp.	3	9.1
Western Union Telegraph	3	9.1
American Communication	3	9.1
Heritage Communication	2	6.1
United Television	2	6.1
United Telecommunication	1	3.0
Emerson Radio	1	3.0

Table 4-15. Medical High Yield Debt Issuers Held by Mutual Funds

Issuer	Number of Funds Holding Issuer	Percent of Total Funds
Republic Health	17	51.5%
Nu-Med	14	42.4
Health Resources Corp. of Am.	11	33.3
Beverly Enterprises	11	33.3
American Healthcare Mgmt.	10	30.3
Westworld Comm. Healthcare	10	30.3
Care Enterprises	8	24.2
Charter Medical Corp.	8	24.2
ICN Pharmaceuticals	7	21.2
Manor Care	6	18.2
Iroquois Brands Ltd.	5	15.2
Paracelsus Healthcare	4	12.1
Mediq Inc.	3	9.1
Patent Tech. Inc.	3	9.1
Bio-Rad Laboratories	3	9.1
National Health	2	6.1
Universal Health Services	2	6.1
American Health Care Intl.	2	6.1
Cordis Corp.	2	6.1

Table 4-15. (*continued*)

Issuer	Number of Funds Holding Issuer	Percent of Total Funds
Health Care International	1	3.0
HPSC Inc.	1	3.0
Bergen Brunswig Corp.	1	3.0

Table 4-16. Utility High Yield Debt Issuers Companies Held by Mutual Funds

Issuer	Number of Funds Holding Issuer	Percent of Total Funds
Consumers Power Co.	24	72.7%
Middle South Energy	24	72.7
Long Island Lighting	23	69.7
Public Service Co. of N.H.	12	36.4
Public Service Co. of Indiana	11	33.3
Louisiana Power & Light Co.	9	27.3
Ohio Edison Co.	8	24.2
Philadelphia Electric	7	21.2
Northwest Pipeline	6	18.2
Arkansas Power & Light	2	6.1
Beaver County, Pennsylvania Industrial Development	1	3.0
South Carolina Ed.	1	3.0
Harris Graphics Corp.	1	3.0
United Illuminating	1	3.0

Table 4-17. Retail High Yield Debt Issuers Held by Mutual Funds

Issuer	Number of Funds Holding Issuer	Percent of Total Funds
Wickes Companies	17	51.5%
Pantry Pride	17	51.5

Issuer	Number of Funds Holding Issuer	Percent of Total Funds
Woodward & Lothrop	13	39.4
McCrory Corp.	11	33.3
Rapid American	10	30.3
Fay's Drug Co.	8	24.2
Palm Beach	7	21.2
Kettle Restaurants	5	15.2
Pier 1 Imports	5	15.2
Cole National	5	15.2
Higbee	3	9.1
Waxman Industries	3	9.1
Hasbro Bradley	3	9.1
McGregor Corp.	3	9.1
Genesco	3	9.1
Town & Country Jewelry	3	9.1
S.E. Nichols Inc.	2	6.1
Montgomery Ward Credit Co.	2	6.1
Circle K Corp.	2	6.1
Dairy Mart Convenience Stores	2	6.1
May Department Stores	1	3.0
Revco	1	3.0

Table 4-18. Airline High Yield Debt Issuers Held by Mutual Funds

Issuer	Number of Funds Holding Issuer	Percent of Total Funds
People Express	19	57.6%
Texas Air Corp.	17	51.5
Eastern Air Lines	14	42.4
Pan American World Airways	13	39.4
Republic Airlines	12	36.4
Western Air Lines	7	21.2
Muse Air Corp.	7	21.2
World Airways	6	18.2

Table 4-18. (*continued*)

Issuer	Number of Funds Holding Issuer	Percent of Total Funds
World Airways	6	18.2
Trans World Airlines	4	12.1
Texas International Airlines	2	6.1
US Air	1	3.0
Frontier Holdings	1	3.0
American West Airline	1	3.0
Midway Airline	1	3.0
US Air Financial N.V.	1	3.0
US Group	1	3.0
Frontier Airlines	1	3.0

Table 4-19. Transportation High Yield Debt Issuers Held by Mutual Funds

Issuer	Number of Funds Holding Issuer	Percent of Total Funds
Chicago & NW. Railway	13	39.4%
Rio Grande Industries	9	27.3
Chicago Pacific	7	21.2
Harvard Industries	7	21.2
Atlas Van Lines	6	18.2
Illinois Central Gulf Railroad	5	15.2
Tiger International	4	12.1
Kinney	2	6.1
Builber's Trans.	2	6.1
Flying Tiger Line	1	3.0
Flexi-Van Co.	1	3.0
Chicago, Milwaukee, St. Paul & Pacific Railroad	1	3.0
Seatrain Lines	1	3.0

Table 4-20. Conglomerate High Yield Debt Issuers Held by Mutual Funds

Issuer	Number of Funds Holding Issuer	Percent of Total Funds
Scovill	9	27.3%
MCO	3	9.1
Farley/Northwest Acq. Corp.	3	9.1
Crane Co.	2	6.1
Clabir	2	6.1
Talley Industries	1	3.0
LaBarge	1	3.0
Zapata Corp.	1	3.0
Allegheny International	1	3.0

OTHER INSTITUTIONAL INVESTORS

As of the end of 1985, four of the five largest institutional investors in the United States were insurance companies. According to *Pension and Investments Age* (January 20, 1986), Prudential Investment Corp. was the biggest with $86.4 billion under management followed by Metropolitan Life ($84.1 billion), Equitable Life Insurance ($77.0 billion), Aetna Life & Casualty Co. ($77.0 billion), and American Express ($63.6 billion). Next in line was the largest broker-dealer Merrill Lynch ($52 billion) followed by Citicorp, Travelers Insurance, Bankers Trust, and TIAA-CREF. The latter is the money manager for most of the nation's college and university professors.

Among the top 100 institutional investors, 21 were insurance companies ($682 billion), 36 were banks and trust companies ($539 billion), 20 investment counseling and mutual fund companies ($314 billion) followed by 14 in-house pension funds controlling $171 billion. All of these institutions represent potential investors, as well as some actual ones, in high yield bonds. We now briefly turn to pension funds.

Pension Fund Investors

Possibly the largest category of investors in high yield debt is the nation's pension funds. We are not aware of any statistics documenting the investments of pension funds in the noninvestment grade market but we would not be surprised if the amount exceeded $20 billion. Indeed, a growing source of investment dollars flowing into high yield bonds are from pension funds. While there are a number of very large public funds, the more frequent high yield investors are private ones. The largest 200 funds had a total of $812 billion invested in 1985. TIAA-CREF was the largest pension fund in 1985 with $37 billion under management. Table 4-21 summarizes the top-10 pension funds with four representing private corporate funds—General Motors, AT&T, General Electric, and IBM. This table also indicates our information about whether the fund had money invested in high yield bonds.

There were over 150 state and corporate pension funds with assets of $1 billion in 1983. Admittedly these are rough estimates, but we estimated that under 2% of the assets of the largest pension funds are now invested in high yield debt. While this relatively small percentage is understandable, given the fiduciary responsibility of such investors, the potential for increased amounts is certainly present. This assumes that the market's image is not severely tarnished and the supply of high yield debt securities continues its impressive growth.

Table 4-21. Ten Largest Pension Funds: 1985

Pension Fund	Asset Size ($ Billions)	Invest in HY Bonds (Yes/No)
TIAA-CREF	$40.0	No
California Public Employees' Retirement System	32.7	Yes
New York State Common Retirement Fund	28.0	No
General Motors	25.1	Yes
New York City Retirement Systems	24.0	No
AT&T	23.3	Yes
General Electric	15.8	No
California State Teachers' Retirement System	15.1	No
New York State Teachers' Retirement System	14.9	No
IBM	13.9	No

Source: *Pension & Investment Age* (January 20, 1986) and discussions with fund managers.

Since pension fund portfolio data is not readily accessible, we can only speculate on the attributes of any high yield bonds they may be holding. We would be surprised if they differed very much from the mutual fund data discussed earlier. For one thing, many of the same mutual fund investment managers are already managing a portion of this country's pension assets. We expect that the same strategies of diversification hold for internally managed pension funds as they prudently attempt to generate higher returns in order to lower annual funding requirements from the parent corporation or organization.

Savings and Loan Associations

A somewhat smaller investor group in the high yield debt market is that of the nation's savings institutions, primarily savings and loan associations. Estimates by the Federal Home Loan Bank Board, in recent (September 1985) testimony before the United States Congress, are that about $6 billion were invested at that time in high yield debt by savings and loans (S&Ls), and that only a very small proportion of these institutions were involved. One S&L, (Columbia S&L in Los Angeles), actually had over $1 billion invested in this market at the end of 1984 and had enjoyed high returns, based on the promised and actual yields of these lower rated instruments (*High Performance*, July 1985).

While it is difficult to estimate savings and loan associations' potential impact on the investing side of the high yield marketplace, it is important to note that the larger institutions are either already involved or beginning to look more seriously at high yield bonds as a viable investment opportunity. Savings and loans have been saddled with large portfolios of low interest mortgage loans. These loans, until recently, locked in the returns on their assets at levels below what new money was costing them. High yield bonds have offered them a way to increase the returns on their assets and so, cut losses. There is, however, some political momentum to limit the level of high yield bond investment that savings and loans can make on the basis of the market's risky profile. This could affect the growth potential in this market from these investors. On the other hand, the Congressional members that we have talked to do not seem inclined to formally restrict federally insured financial institutions.

Debate on Restricting S&L Investments. A number of Congressional committees have been holding hearings and soliciting testimony as to the wisdom of further restrictions on investments in high yield debt. An important concern of these hearings has focused on the nation's federally insured financial institutions, in particular, those already struggling to survive. The primary argument presented in favor of tighter restrictions is the speculative nature of such investments and the fact that public money is potentially at risk by providing insurance through the Federal Savings and Loan Insurance Corporation (FSLIC).

One of the authors recently argued, in testimony before the House Subcommittee on General Oversight and Investigations of the Committee on Banking, Finance and Urban Affairs (September 19, 1985), that based on historical risk-return performance of high yield bond portfolios, it is difficult to support the idea that federally insured institutions should be barred from investing in junk bonds. While the default rate on high yield debt is no doubt higher than on all corporate debt, it does not appear to be any higher, on average, than typical commercial loan portfolios.

One possible solution would be to treat investments in high yield debt, indeed in any risky assets, in the same way that traditional loans are handled by thrift and other lending institutions. Default risk on loans for real estate development, home mortgages, commercial, and consumer purposes are "handled" by setting aside capital reserves to cover expected losses. It would make sense to treat all investments, including those in securities, in a similar manner. Where risk of default is present and can be fairly measured, this information could be used to establish the size of reserves. Coincidentally, the net default rate loss of 1%, discussed in Chapter 5, is approximately the same as recent commercial bank loan loss reserves.

A policy of setting aside additional reserves would, of course, discourage investments in junk bonds by institutions that have a shaky capital base. But that is precisely the kind of institution that is now of such concern to public regulators.

In addition to loan loss reserves on high yield bond investments, we certainly endorse the concept of adequate diversification to ensure that S&Ls realize average return and risk performance. Bookstaber and Jacob (1985) found that adequate diversification in high yield debt could involve as few as 15 individual issuers. We would go so far as to suggest combining diversification principles with a prudent credit quality assessment of individual issues and industrial segments. The concept of quality–junk portfolios for prudent, high yield investing is particularly relevant for S&Ls and will be discussed in Chapters 6, 8, and 9.

Insurance Company Investors

According to A.M. Best Inc., there were 78 insurance companies that had bond holdings of over $1 billion each in 1984, with Metropolitan Life and Prudential holding $31.3 billion and $23.6 billion. Higher bond returns help to boost profitability and protect against unforeseen contingencies, and while no high yield debt investment figures exist, the high yield debt area may become attractive to insurance portfolio managers. Also, as activity in the private placement market is supplanted by public high yield bond issuances, the pressure to participate will grow. Some individual state insurance regulators (e.g., New York), are presently grappling with the question of whether or not to restrict investments in junk bonds.

Remaining Investor Groups

The institutional investors previously listed are not the only actual or potential participants on the buy side. Other groups include specialized closed-end funds and trusts that have as their goal to take advantage of special situations. These include such areas as private debt, options and futures, turn-around situations, bankrupt debt and equity, as well as the increasingly common original-issue-junk-bond. The reader is cautioned to examine these institutions' prospectuses very carefully so as to understand the risk-return objectives and techniques for achieving them.

Finally, private individuals, corporations, investment banks, and subsidiaries of commercial banks round out the list of major investors in high yield debt. As the risks and returns in this market become increasingly quantifiable, the number and scope of investing participants should increase. At the same time, increased restrictions on investing in junk bonds and/or the occurrence of extremely adverse default rate experience in the future would certainly retard investor interest, which in turn would reduce the ability to place new issues.

5

Default Rates
On High Yield Debt

SUMMARY OF FINDINGS

High yield bond investors in the past have experienced healthy return premiums over investment grade securities, but they have also experienced substantial defaults. Without a reliable measure of past losses from defaults, investors cannot intelligently estimate the net returns over time on high yield bonds. This chapter provides an in-depth and comprehensive look at the default experience since the dramatic growth of the high yield bond market began.

Default rates can be measured using several different base levels or denominators (i.e., total public debt, total straight debt, low-rated debt, etc.). The default rates discussed here (except where noted) were derived by dividing the par value of low rated defaulting debt by the total low-rated, straight debt outstanding. We found that the default rate on high yield bonds from 1974 to 1985 averaged 1.53% (or 153 basis points annually). Year-to-year variations in this rate were substantial. This default level is significantly higher than rates generated using *total* straight debt outstanding as the base, that is, 0.09 of 1% for the same period. We feel the higher rate is much more relevant to investors with portfolios in the high yield area since virtually all defaults occur in the low-rated segment of the corporate debt market. It is true, however, that certain high current yield investors, for example, mutual funds, invest in both investment grade and also junk bonds. In their case, some weighted average of default rates would be even more relevant.

The *actual losses* from default, are somewhat lower than these rates would imply. Defaulted bonds, far from becoming valueless, traded, on average, at 41% of par shortly after default over our sample period (44% in 1985). After accounting for the bonds' retained value and the loss of interest, the average reduction in returns to the investor would have been in the 96 to 101 basis point range annually, assuming purchase at par. The net default rate in 1985 was exactly 100 BP or 1%. The recent (1978 to 1984) net returns, however, on high yield debt have been very impressive, averaging 583 BPs above the long-term government bond index—and these compound rates of return are measured after default. The 1978 to 1985 differential was lower at 270 BP.

We will also look at industry segments that may be especially prone to default. Railroads and real estate investment trusts were vulnerable in the past, but are unlikely to represent a large portion of future defaults. Retailer, electronic/computer, airline, and most recently, oil and gas company defaults have become more common in recent years. The latter industrial sector was particularly hard hit in 1985 and again in early 1986. One recent record default, LTV Corp. (July 1986), shows the vulnerability of the steel industry. LTV, the largest bankruptcy ever, swelled the 1986 gross default rate to almost 3% by mid-year.

WHAT BASE TO USE

Most of the past studies which have estimated or documented the default experience of U.S. corporate debt have dealt with the entire public corporate debt market, estimated to be almost $400 billion by mid-1985 (Table 5-1) and over $425 billion by year-end. These studies, including the classic Hickman (1958) study, the Atkinson (1967) update, and the Hill-Post (1978) analysis of lower-rated debt noted that the total default rate of United States corporate debt ranged from 0.03% during 1960 to 1967 to 3.2% during 1930 to 1939. Table 5-2 summarizes the results from a number of disparate studies on the default experience since 1900. We caution the reader as to the direct comparability of these default rates since the bases used are not identical and the degree of comprehensiveness is not always clear.

We believe that the appropriate base to calculate the default rate for high yield corporate debt is the low-rated, straight debt market. If the strategy entails investing in this sector (and nearly all corporate defaults occur here), then the relevant rate should be based on this sector's outstanding debt amounts. We rarely observe a bond defaulting when its bond rating is investment grade (BBB-/Baa3 or higher) just prior to default. Out of 143 defaulting firms from the 16-year period 1970–1985, only four had a rating of BBB/Baa3 or higher six months prior to default. (Johns Manville's two issues had the only A rating.)

It is possible, however, for a debt issue to become very illiquid while still investment grade. If it subsequently defaults after being downgraded to noninvestment grade status, then an argument can be made that the investor was "locked-in" while still in the so-called investment grade status. We have been told that this was the case for one of the Baldwin United issues.

Table 5-1. Public Straight Debt Outstanding 1970 to 1985 ($MM)

Year	Par Value Public Straight Debt Outstanding Over Year[a]	Low Rated Debt[b]			
		Straight Public Debt	Percent of Public Straight Debt	Amount Outstanding Per Issuer	Amount Outstanding Per Issue
1985	$395,500 (est.)	$59,078	14.9%	$135	$55
1984	363,300	41,700	11.5	125	49
1983	339,850	28,223	8.3	93	39
1982	320,850	18,536	5.8	69	33
1981	303,800	17,362	5.7	62	32
1980	282,000	15,125	5.4	59	31
1979	260,600	10,675	4.1	47	30
1978	245,000	9,401	3.8	49	30
1977	228,500	8,479	3.7	46	27
1976	209,900	8,015	3.8	41	27
1975	187,900	7,720	4.1	41	27
1974	167,000	11,101[d]	6.6	59	35
1973	154,800[c]	8,082	5.2	45	29
1972	145,700	7,106	4.9	45	29
1971	132,500	6,643	5.0	45	29
1970	116,200	6,996	6.0	48	32

[a] Average of beginning and ending years' figures (1975 to 1985).
[b] Source: Standard & Poor's Bond Guide and Moody's Bond Record, July issues of each year. Defaulted railroads excluded. Also includes nonrated debt equivalent to rated debt for low-rated firms.
[c] Estimates for 1973 and earlier based on linear regression of this column vs. the Federal Reserve's Corporate Bonds Outstanding figures (Federal Reserve Bulletin.)
[d] Includes $2.7 billion in Con Edison debt.

Table 5-2.   Corporate Debt Default Rates, 1900 to 1985

Period	Total Corporate Debt Default Rate
1900–1909	0.90%
1910–1919	2.00
1920–1929	1.00
1930–1939	3.20
1940–1949	0.40
1950–1959	0.04
1960–1967	0.03
1968–1977	0.16
1978–1985	0.10

Sources: Hickman (1958), Atkinson (1967), Fitzpatrick and Severiens (1978), Hill and Post (1978) and calculated by the authors.

There has never been a default involving a triple-A original issue bond and only 9 defaulting issues that were A-rated or double-A. A review of the details of the prior-rating experience for defaulted debt appears at a later point in this chapter.

It could be argued that a more relevant default rate base would be all low-rated public straight debt *less* utilities, because defaults have occurred only in the nonutility segment. This base, being a smaller one (see Table 5-3), would result in higher default rates. In recent years, however, downgraded utilities have become a relatively large segment of the high yield straight debt area. In mid-1985, utilities accounted for about 20% of this market, although, by year-end 1985, the proportion fell to 15.6% and to just 5.0% by April 30, 1986. While there have been no utility defaults to date, the notion is not nearly as inconceivable as it formerly was. On balance, the increased risk and size of the utility

Table 5-3.   Low-Rated Public Straight Debt Outstanding Less Utilities^a ($MM)

Year	Low Rated Debt Less Utilities	Percent of Total Public Straight Debt	Amount Outstanding Per Issuer	Amount Outstanding Per Issue
1985	$47,190	11.9%	$112	$56
1984	32,120	8.6	101	51
1983	22,167	6.5	76	40
1982	16,111	5.0	62	35
1981	15,010	4.9	56	35
1980	12,807	4.5	52	34
1979	10,031	3.8	47	30
1978	8,995	3.7	49	31
1977	7,548	3.3	47	31
1976	7,024	3.3	42	29
1975	6,971	3.7	43	30
1974	7,445	4.5	45	32
1973	7,195	4.6	42	32
1972	6,245	4.3	45	31
1971	5,935	4.5	45	31
1970	6,448	5.5	48	32

Source: Standard & Poor's Bond Guide and *Moody's Bond Record,* July issues (June amounts) of each year. Defaulted railroads excluded. Also includes nonrated debt equivalent to rated debt for low-rated firms. 1985 totals include $5.97 billion of exchange debt.
^a See Table 5–1 for total straight public debt dollar amounts, 842 nonutility issues outstanding in July 1985 and 420 issuers. There was $11.88 billion of utility high yield debt in July, 1985.

market, plus the need to use a consistent base over time, we believe, warrant the inclusion of the utility sector in the default rate base.

The outstanding amounts used in this analysis were calculated using July issues of *Standard & Poor's Bond Guide* and *Moody's Bond Record.* Various prior studies have used different points in the year for calculating the amount outstanding. If we had used year-end totals instead of mid-year amounts, the default rate for 1974 to 1985 would be 10 to 15 basis points *lower*. Mid-year figures were used here since technical defaults on any new issues would not take place until at least the initial coupon payments were due (unless bankruptcy or defaults on other issues took place). This would mean that semiannual coupon bonds issued after June of any year, generally, could not default (by missing a coupon payment), until the next calendar year. The dollars outstanding for each default came from the bond guides for the month when the firm fell into a D (DDD in earlier years) rating category or, where no rating was found, the bankruptcy filing date.

THE RESULTS

The 16-year period between 1970 and 1985 witnessed the default of over $4.6 billion of straight debt and $6.6 billion of total debt (see Table 5-4 and Exhibit 5-1). For a comprehensive listing of the 143 firms (77 of which had public straight debt) that defaulted, the dates of default, and the aggregate amounts of defaulted debt per company, see Table 5-5. The actual number of defaulting issuers is somewhat larger since we combined subsidiaries with parent companies.

The relevant timespan to consider in calculating the default rate, we believe, is the 1974 to 1985 period. The straight, low-rated debt marketplace from 1970 to 1977 was made up primarily of declining, exinvestment grade firms. Few, if any, new issues were rated less than BBB (Baa) and there was limited liquidity or interest in the low-rated area. The more "modern era" of high yield investing began in the late 1970s when low-rated, new issuers appeared and the mar-

Table 5-4.   Public Corporate Debt Defaulting on Interest and/or Principal: 1970 to 1985[a] ($MM)

Year of Default	Straight Debt	Convertible Debt	Total Debt in Default
1985	$ 992.10	$ 310.02	$1,302.12
1984	344.16	279.95	624.11
1983	301.08	111.55	412.63
1982	752.34[b]	243.29	995.63[b]
1981	27.00	52.61	79.61
1980	224.11	31.60	255.71
1979	20.00	10.70	30.70
1978	118.90	73.30	192.20
1977	380.57	74.21	454.78
1976	29.51	83.99	113.50
1975	204.10	115.63	319.73
1974	122.82	165.87	288.69
1973	49.07	150.84	199.91
1972	193.25	79.34	272.59
1971	82.00	42.90	124.90
1970	796.71	135.81	932.52
Total	$4,637.72	$1,961.61	$6,599.33

[a] See Table 5–8 for details. Includes those issues whose rating dropped to D due to missed interest payments but did not legally default. The amount of legal defaults in 1985 was $402.40 million.
[b] Includes $175 million in Johns Manville debt which was rated investment grade prior to default.

ket began to expand. While the market had not changed appreciably by 1974, the first of two major recessions in our timespan (1974 to 1975 and 1981 to 1982) had begun. Including both recessions gives investors a more realistic feel for the default experiernce, as these downturns conceivably represent the magnitude of economic shocks that could recur in the future. Also, the bulk of the railroad defaults had occurred by 1974. For these reasons, we believe 1974 to be

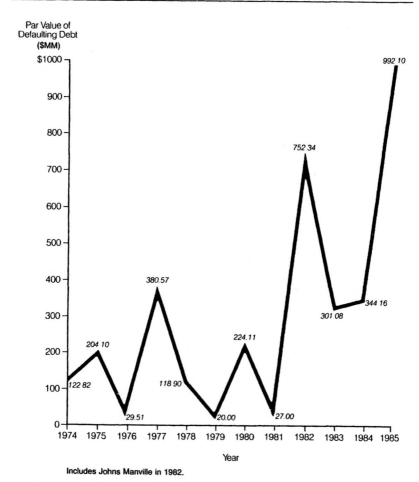

Par Value of
Defaulting Debt
($MM)

Exhibit 5-1   Public straight debt defaulting. Includes all issues involving firms that missed an interest payment.

an appropriate starting point for measuring default rates relevant to today's marketplace. It should be noted that the 1974–1985 default experience is slightly higher than the more recent period, 1978–1985, when the market began to expand rapidly.

From 1974 to 1985, the default rate on straight, low-rated

Table 5-5. Companies Defaulting on Debt: 1970 to 1985[a] ($MM)

Default Date	Company	Bankruptcy Filing Date	Straight Debt	Convertible Debt	Total Debt
2/70	Chic. Milw. & St. Paul RR	12/77	$ 0.00	$ 31.10	$ 31.10
2/70	Roberts Co.	2/70	5.03	0.00	5.03
3/70	Boston & Maine RR	3/70	46.30	0.00	46.30
5/70	Farrington Mfg.	1/71	0.00	3.80	3.80
6/70	Airlift International	6/81	0.00	19.00	19.00
6/70	Penn Central Trans. & Subs.	6/70	618.18	0.00	618.18
7/70	Visual Electronics	7/70	0.00	1.71	1.71
7/70	Clev. C&C St. L. RR	7/70	76.50	0.00	76.50
7/70	Lehigh Valley RR	7/70	50.70	0.00	50.70
8/70	Fairfield Technology	8/70	0.00	2.00	2.00
9/70	Computer Application	10/71	0.00	18.60	18.60
11/70	Elcor Chemical	7/71	0.00	12.40	12.40
12/70	Ozark Airlines	—	0.00	22.20	22.20
12/70	Viatron Computer	2/71	0.00	25.00	25.00
	Subtotal for year		796.71	135.81	932.52
3/71	Mohawk Airlines	—	0.00	8.00	8.00
6/71	King Resources	6/71	0.00	24.40	24.40
7/71	Waltham Ind.	7/71	0.00	8.00	8.00
10/71	Great Markwestern	10/71	0.00	2.50	2.50
11/71	Reading Railroad	11/71	82.00	0.00	82.00
	Subtotal for year		82.00	42.90	124.90

2/72	FAS Intl.	2/72	0.00	16.34	16.34
6/72	Erie RR and Subs.	6/72	187.50	0.00	187.50
8/72	American Export Ind.	—	0.00	60.00	60.00
11/72	Harvard Ind.	11/72	5.75	3.00	8.75
	Subtotal for year		193.25	79.34	272.59
1/73	DCA Development	2/73	0.00	3.80	3.80
3/73	Sherwood Leasing	3/73	0.00	12.90	12.90
3/73	Esgro Inc.	3/73	0.00	5.84	5.84
4/73	Equity Funding of America	4/73	22.00	61.40	83.40
5/73	Arlan's Dept. Stores	5/73	0.00	15.50	15.50
7/73	Lyntex Corp.	7/73	0.00	13.80	13.80
7/73	U.S. Fin. Services	7/73	0.00	35.00	35.00
9/73	Arden Mayfair	—	21.90	0.00	21.90
10/73	Ann Arbor Mich. RR	10/73	5.17	0.00	5.17
12/73	Parkview-GEM	12/73	0.00	2.60	2.60
	Subtotal for year		49.07	150.84	199.91
2/74	Westgate-California	2/74	7.60	16.40	24.00
3/74	Boothe Computer	—	0.00	17.90	17.90
4/74	Electro Space	4/74	0.00	9.99	9.99
5/74	Interstate Dept. Stores	5/74	0.00	20.44	20.44
6/74	Wolf Corp.	—	3.53	0.00	3.53
7/74	Omega-Alpha Corp.	9/74	25.00	0.00	25.00

[a] The "Default Date" indicates the date when the company's S&P rating was changed to a D, DD or DDD, or (where the company's debt was not listed or rated by S&P) its filing date, whichever came first. Amounts outstanding ($ in millions) are at or near default dates and come from S&P, Moody's or annual reports.

Table 5-5. Companies Defaulting on Debt: 1970 to 1985[a] ($MM) *(Continued)*

Default Date	Company	Bankruptcy Filing Date	Straight Debt	Convertible Debt	Total Debt
7/74	Bohack Corp.	7/74	$ 0.00	$ 3.69	$ 3.69
10/74	National Bella Hess	10/74	0.00	3.70	3.70
10/74	Investors Funding	10/74	49.49	90.76	140.25
11/74	Continental Investment	4/76	37.20	1.67	38.87
12/74	Career Academy Inc.	12/74	0.00	1.32	1.32
	Subtotal for year		122.82	165.87	288.69
1/75	Fidelity Mortgage Inv.	1/75	0.00	2.75	2.75
2/75	Daylin Inc.	2/75	53.30	0.00	53.30
3/75	Chicago, R.I. & Pac. RR	3/75	47.50	0.00	47.50
3/75	Gray Mfg.	3/75	0.00	2.38	2.38
5/75	Hallcraft Homes	—	0.00	15.00	15.00
7/75	National Telephone	7/75	0.00	2.50	2.50
10/75	Grant, W.T.	10/75	24.00	93.00	117.00
11/75	GAC Property Credit	12/75	79.30	0.00	79.30
	Subtotal for year		204.10	115.63	319.73
1/76	Optical Scanning	3/76	0.00	5.42	5.42
3/76	Continental Mtge. Investors	3/76	0.00	36.00	36.00
5/76	Sanitas Service	5/76	0.00	8.20	8.20
7/76	Permaneer Corp.	6/76	0.00	13.17	13.17
8/76	Colwell Mortgage & Trust	2/78	25.00	0.00	25.00

114

9/76	Duplan Corp.	9/76	0.00	21.20	21.20
10/76	Treco Inc.	—	4.51	0.00	4.51
	Subtotal for year		29.51	83.99	113.50
2/77	Wyly Corp.	—	0.00	19.60	19.60
2/77	Justice Mtge.	1/78	19.60	0.00	19.60
3/77	Great American Mtge. & Trust	3/77	50.00	0.00	50.00
5/77	Grolier Inc.	—	30.00	22.50	52.50
7/77	United Merchants & Mfg.	7/77	48.50	19.50	68.00
7/77	Guardian Mtge. Inv.	3/78	33.00	0.21	33.21
8/77	First Mtge. Inv.	—	28.80	0.00	28.80
9/77	Tri-South Mtge.	—	11.40	0.00	11.40
12/77	Chic. Milw. St. P. & Pac. RR & Subs.	12/77	146.37	0.00	146.37
	Subtotal for year		367.67	61.81	429.48
3/78	Frigitemp	3/78	0.00	5.00	5.00
3/78	Commonwealth Oil	3/78	0.00	17.90	17.90
5/78	Chase Manhattan Mtge.	2/79	77.60	30.90	108.50
10/78	Food Fair Corp.	10/78	41.30	0.00	41.30
11/78	Allied Supermarkets	11/78	0.00	19.50	19.50
	Subtotal for year		118.90	73.30	192.20
4/79	American Reserve	4/80	0.00	7.60	7.60

[a] The "Default Date" indicates the date when the company's S&P rating was changed to a D, DD or DDD, or (where the company's debt was not listed or rated by S&P) its filing date, whichever came first. Amounts outstanding ($ in millions) are at or near default dates and come from S&P, Moody's or annual reports.

Table 5-5. Companies Defaulting on Debt: 1970 to 1985[a] (Continued)

Default Date	Company	Bankruptcy Filing Date	Straight Debt	Convertible Debt	Total Debt
4/79	Allied Artists	4/79	$ 0.00	$ 3.10	$ 3.10
10/79	Inforex	10/79	20.00	0.00	20.00
	Subtotal for year		20.00	10.70	30.70
1/80	Dasa Corp.	—	0.00	2.55	2.55
4/80	Penn-Dixie Ind.	4/80	0.00	9.00	9.00
7/80	Itel Corp.	1/81	184.60	0.00	184.60
9/80	White Motor	9/80	23.31	6.75	30.06
10/80	Combustion Equip.	10/80	16.20	13.30	29.50
	Subtotal for year		224.11	31.60	255.71
2/81	Seatrain Lines	2/81	0.00	50.00	50.00
10/81	FSC Inc.	10/81	7.00	2.61	9.61
12/81	American Communications	12/81	20.00	0.00	20.00
	Subtotal for year		27.00	52.61	79.61
1/82	Morton Shoes Inc.	1/82	11.50	0.00	11.50
2/82	South Atlantic Financial	10/82	16.90	0.00	16.90
2/82	Rusco Ind.	2/82	0.00	6.19	6.19
2/82	Lional Corp.	2/82	15.00	0.00	15.00
3/82	Mego International	3/82	14.10	0.00	14.10
3/82	California Life Fin.	—	20.00	0.00	20.00
4/82	Wickes/Gambles Skogmo/Credit	4/82	263.04	28.10	291.14

4/82	Standard Packaging/Saxon	11.10	32.70	43.80
4/82	Spector Ind. (Div. of Telecom)	0.00	3.00	3.00
4/82	AM International	37.00	11.00	48.00
5/82	Braniff Airlines	133.70	0.00	133.70
7/82	Nucorp Energy	0.00	110.00	110.00
8/82	Johns Manville Corp.	175.00	0.00	175.00
9/82	Shelter Resources	0.00	11.00	11.00
10/82	Revere Copper & Brass	0.00	41.30	41.30
11/82	Telecom Corp.	25.00	0.00	25.00
12/82	Amarex	30.00	0.00	30.00
	Subtotal for year	752.34	243.29	995.63
2/83	Regency Investors	0.00	17.20	17.20
3/83	Marion Corp.	0.00	20.00	20.00
4/83	Wilson Foods	45.70	0.00	45.70
4/83	Texas General Resources	30.00	0.00	30.00
12/83	MFG Oil Corp.	75.00	0.00	75.00
—	Flight Transportation	25.00	0.00	25.00
8/83	Pioneer Texas (DPA)	0.00	4.50	4.50
7/83	Hardwick Co.	6.00	0.00	6.00
10/83	Phoenix Steel Corp.	0.00	4.85	4.85
8/83	Peninsula Resources	0.00	15.00	15.00
9/83	Cont'l Air/Texas Intl. Air.	47.84	47.29	95.13
9/83	Baldwin-United/DH Baldwin	46.20	0.00	46.20

a The "Default Date" indicates the date when the company's S&P rating was changed to a D, DD or DDD, or (where the company's debt was not listed or rated by S&P) its filing date, whichever came first. Amounts outstanding ($ in millions) are at or near default dates and come from S&P, Moody's or annual reports.

Table 5–5. Companies Defaulting on Debt: 1970 to 1985ª (Continued)

Default Date	Company	Bankruptcy Filing Date	Straight Debt	Convertible Debt	Total Debt
9/83	Altec Corp.	9/83	$ 7.84	$ 0.00	$ 7.84
11/83	Anglo Energy	11/83	17.50	0.00	17.50
	Subtotal for year		301.08	108.84	409.92
1/84	Anacomp	1/84	0.00	50.00	50.00
3/84	Pizza Time Theater	3/84	0.00	50.00	50.00
4/84	Page Petroleum	—	0.00	25.00	25.00
4/84	Emons	4/84	27.30	0.00	27.30
4/84	Charter Co.	4/84	106.10	0.00	106.10
6/84	Tomlinson Oil	6/84	0.00	15.65	15.65
7/84	Land Resources	—	0.00	16.30	16.30
7/84	Commonwealth Oil	7/84	0.00	40.00	40.00
10/84	Transcontinental Energy	10/84	5.44	0.00	5.44
10/84	Kenai Corp.	—	27.50	0.00	27.50
11/84	Storage Tech./Documation	11/84	131.00	83.00	214.00
12/84	North American Car	12/84	46.82	0.00	46.82
	Subtotal for year		344.16	279.95	624.11
2/85	American Quasar Petroleum	—	65.00	0.00	65.00
3/85	Oak Industries	—	0.00	100.00	100.00
4/85	Castle & Cooke	—	100.00	19.42	119.42
4/85	Peninsula Resources	—	0.00	15.00	15.00
5/85	Oxoco Inc.	—	65.00	0.00	65.00

		Default Date			
6/85	Punta Gorda Isles	—	0.00	12.09	12.09
6/85	Hunt Int'l Resources Corp.	3/85	31.40	0.00	31.40
7/85	Sharon Steel	—	60.00	0.00	60.00
8/85	Tacoma Boatbuilding	9/85	0.00	13.10	13.10
9/85	Buttes Gas and Oil	11/85	105.00	0.00	105.00
9/85	Beker Industries	10/85	65.00	0.00	65.00
9/85	Global Marine	1/86	275.00	123.00	398.00
11/85	Brock Hotel	—	44.50	0.00	44.50
11/85	Macrodyne Industries	—	0.00	13.21	13.21
11/85	Pettibone Corp.	—	20.00	0.00	20.00
12/85	Elsinore Corp./Finance	—	140.00	0.00	140.00
12/85	Delmed	—	0.00	14.20	14.20
12/85	Mission Insurance	—	21.20	0.00	21.20
	Subtotal for Year		992.10	310.02	1,302.12
	Total debt defaulted		$4,624.82	$1,946.50	$6,571.32

a The "Default Date" indicates the date when the company's S&P rating was changed to a D, DD or DDD, or (where the company's debt was not listed or rated by S&P) its filing date, whichever came first. Amounts outstanding ($ in millions) are at or near default dates and come from S&P, Moody's or annual reports.

Table 5-6. Historical Default Rates—Low Rated, Straight Debt Only[a] ($MM)

Year	Par Value Outstanding with Utilities[b]	Par Value Defaulted	Default Rate (%)	Par Value Public Outstanding Less Utilities[b]	Default Rate(%)
1985	$59,078	$992.10	1.679%	$47,190	2.102%
1984	41,700	344.16	0.825	32,120	1.071
1983	28,233	301.08	1.066	22,167	1.358
1982	18,536	577.34	3.115	16,111	3.584
1981	17,362	27.00	0.155	15,010	0.180
1980	15,126	224.11	1.482	12,807	1.750
1979	10,675	20.00	0.187	10,031	0.199
1978	9,401	118.90	1.265	8,995	1.322
1977	8,479	380.57	4.488	7,548	5.042
1976	8,015	29.51	0.368	7,024	0.420
1975	7,720	204.10	2.644	6,971	2.928
1974	11,101[c]	122.82	1.106	7,445	1.650
1973	8,082	49.07	0.607	7,195	0.682
1972	7,106	193.25	2.719	6,245	3.094
1971	6,643	82.00	1.234	5,935	1.382
1970	6,996	796.71	11.388	6,448	12.356
Average default rate—1970 to 1985:			2.146%		2.445%
Average default rate—1974 to 1985:			**1.532%[d]**		**1.800%**
Average default rate—1978 to 1985:			1.222%		1.446%

[a] Issues rated below Baa3 by Moody's or BBB – by Standard & Poor's. Includes nonrated debt of issuers with other equivalently rated issues. The default rate includes issues whose bond rating fell to D due to a missed interest payment but may not have legally defaulted.
[b] Source: Standard & Poor's Bond Guide and Moody's Bond Record, July issues of each year.
[c] Includes almost $2.7 billion of Consolidated Edison Co. debt.
[d] Does not include Johns Manville, as it was an investment grade default. If included, the 1974–1985 rate would have been 1.61%.

120

debt ranged from 0.16 of 1% in 1981 to 4.49% in 1977, with the average annual rate being 1.53% of par value (Table 5-6 and Exhibit 5-2). One defaulting company, Johns Manville, was investment grade at the time of default and so was not included. (The rate using the nonutility base mentioned earlier, for the same period, was 1.80%.) Traditional analysis using the total of public straight debt outstanding as a base results in a default rate of 0.09 of 1% (1974 to 1985) or about ¹⁄₁₆th of what we view as the relevant rate. (See Table 5-7 for

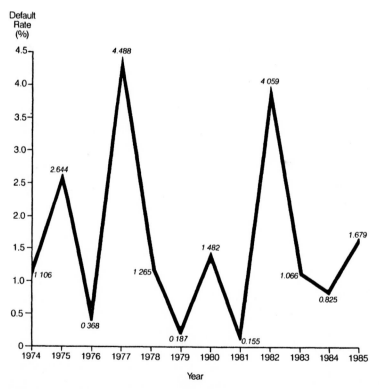

Exhibit 5-2 Public straight debt default rate. As % of high yield debt outstanding. Includes Johns Manville. If these issues were not included, the 1982 default rate would have been 3.115%.

average default rates on total corporate debt for various time periods.)

The straight debt default rate for the entire period, 1970–1985, was 2.15% (Table 5-6). This rate is considerably higher than the aforementioned levels because of the 1970 Penn Central default. With Penn Central, the default rate for 1970 was 11.4%. Without it, the 1970 rate falls to 2.5% (almost all of which was other railroads).

The number of firms that defaulted on either straight or convertible debt over the 1974 to 1985 period ranged from 18 in 1985 to 3 in both 1979 and 1981 (Table 5-8). Since 1982, the number of firms defaulting has risen to 12 or more in each year; something one might expect as the number of issuers grows dramatically. The 1985 totals for both number of firms and dollar amounts marked the high year for the 1970 to 1985 period. Keep in mind that the number of firms and dollars in the entire market were substantially greater in 1985 than in previous years and the default *rate* of 1.68% in that year, while above average for the period under study, was considerably lower than it was in 1977 and 1982.

The number of firms defaulting relative to total issuers with outstanding high yield debt may also be of interest to investors. Table 5-9 lists the approximate number of rated, high yield, straight debt issuers outstanding for each year for the 16-year period. It also highlights the default rate in issuer terms. The number of issuers outstanding increased from 145 in 1970 to 190 in 1978, and to 435 in 1985. The percentage of defaulting issuers ranged from 0.4% in 1979 to 4.3% in 1977. Over the 1974 to 1985 period, the issuer default rate was 2.1%. Prior to 1985 it appeared that the issuer default rate was dropping as the number of issuers increased. The last year's results reverses that trend. Overall, the issuer default rate is high relative to the dollar default rate highlighted earlier.

Table 5–7. Historical Default Rates—All Ratings ($MM)

Year	Par Value of Straight and Convertible Public Debt Outstanding[a]	Par Value of all Public Defaults[c]	Default Rate	Par Value Public Straight Debt Outstanding[a]	Par Value of Straight Debt Defaulted[c]	Default Rate
1985	$459,300(est.)	$1302.02	.283%	$428,300(est.)	$992.10	.232%
1984	413,200	624.11	.151	391,700	344.16	.088
1983	372,900	412.63	.111	350,500	301.08	.086
1982	352,300	995.63	.283	329,200	752.34	.228
1981	331,400	79.61	.023	312,500	27.00	.009
1980	311,900	255.71	.082	295,100	224.11	.076
1979	281,700	30.70	.011	269,900	20.00	.007
1978	258,600	192.20	.074	252,200	118.90	.047
1977	248,300	454.78	.183	237,800	380.57	.160
1976	229,100	113.50	.049	219,200	29.51	.013
1975	209,900	319.73	.152	200,600	204.10	.102
1974	183,500	288.69	.157	175,200	122.82	.070
1973	162,900[b]	199.91	.123	158,800[b]	49.07	.031
1972	154,400	272.59	.176	150,900	193.25	.128
1971	143,000	124.90	.087	140,500	82.00	.058
1970	125,500	932.52	.743	124,400	796.71	.640
	Average default rate—1970 to 1985:		.168%			.123%
	Average default rate—1974 to 1985:		.130%			.093%
	Average default rate—1978 to 1985:		.127%			.097%

[a] These numbers are year end and outstanding amounts.
[b] Estimates for 1973 and earlier based on linear regression of this column vs. the Federal Reserve's Corporate Bonds Outstanding figures (Federal Reserve Bulletin).
[c] For details on default amounts, see Table 5–8.

123

Table 5-8.　Number of Companies with Public Debt Defaulting[a]

Year	Nonrailroad Companies	Major Railroads
1985	18	—
1984	12	—
1983	14	—
1982	17	—
1981	3	—
1980	5	—
1979	3	—
1978	5	—
1977	8	1
1976	7	—
1975	7	1
1974	11	—
1973	9	1
1972	3	1
1971	4	1
1979	9	5
Total	135^b	10^b

[a] Includes straight and convertible defaults.
[b] Includes one company that defaulted twice over the period.

While the issuer default rate trend is not clear, the number of dollars defaulting per issuer is increasing. Exhibit 5-3 shows the yearly average defaults per firm (from a low of $14 million in 1981 to $83 million in 1985). The average over the 1974 to 1985 period was $44 million per company default. We anticipate this average will probably continue to increase in the future as the debt outstanding per company increases.

It should be noted that the total dollars and firms in default listed in Table 5-8 are conservative (high) estimates from the investor's viewpoint. At least 24 of these defaulting

Table 5–9. Percent of Low Rated Firms in Default—Straight Debt Only

Year	Number of Low Rated Firms	Number of Firms in Default[a]	Percent in Default
1985	435	12	2.8%
1984	335	6	1.8
1983	305	9	3.0
1982	270	11	4.1
1981	280	2	0.7
1980	255	3	1.2
1979	230	1	0.4
1978	190	2	1.1
1977	185	8	4.3
1976	195	2	1.0
1975	190	4	2.1
1974	190	5	2.6
1973	180	3	1.7
1972	160	2	1.2
1971	150	1	0.7
1970	145	5	3.4

Average percent of low rated firms in default:	1970 to 1985:		1.9%
	1974 to 1985:		2.1%
	1978 to 1985:		2.0%

[a] Public, straight debt defaults only (excludes Johns Manville).

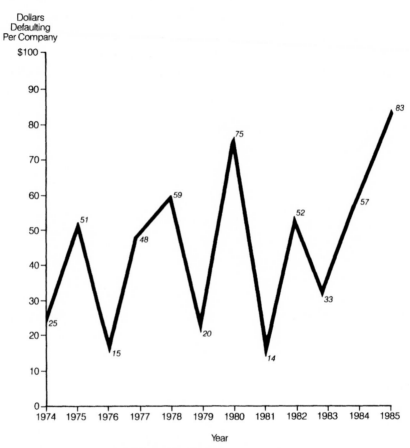

Dollars
Defaulting
Per Company

' For public, low rated straight debt only. Does not include Johns Manville in 1982.

Exhibit 5-3   Average $ defaulting per company. Based on par value at default. For public straight debt only.

firms did not actually file for bankruptcy. In several cases, interest was paid in arrears at a later date either by the firm or by a firm purchasing the defaulted entity. In others, agreements were reached with creditors to restructure the debt. Still, in most cases the price of the outstanding issue dropped dramatically, even if a formal bankruptcy or default did not take place.

IMPACT ON ANNUAL RETURNS

One might conclude that an investor with a portfolio of representative high yield bonds suffered an average annual loss of 153 basis points from the total annual return of the portfolio over the 1974 to 1985 period. (Recall the average default rate was 1.53%.) The average default rate would be the relevant loss only if the security's value fell to zero upon news of the default and the investor liquidated after having puchased at par. In actuality, the prices of debt issues immediately after default can be quite substantial. We found the average price to be 41% of par value. This is based on a study of 56 straight, defaulted debt issues over the 1974 to 1984 period with the price taken at the end of the month in which either the default or bankruptcy occurred, whichever came first. The 1985 average price just after default was 44% (Table 5-10) based on the price of 14 issues. The median price was lower at 38%. If we include the 1985 experience with the 1974–1984 rate, the average was 41.6%—just slightly above the 41% average previously noted. This finding is consistent with the 40 to 43% range that Hickman (1958) found for defaults from 1900 to 1943.

What then is the net impact on investor returns? If the investor sold the bonds just after default, the actual loss would have been 59% of par value, plus roughly one-half of the annual coupon amount (since defaults usually occur

Table 5–10. 1985 Net Default Rate

Company	End of Default Month Price	Coupon Rate (%)	Amount ($MM)
American Quasar	36	14.00	$ 65.0
Oxoco Inc. (A)	37⅞	15.75	40.0
Oxoco Inc. (B)	38	12.86 (Variable Rate)	25.0
Hunt International Resources	12⅜	9.87	31.4
Sharon Steel	54	14.25	60.0
Buttes Gas & Oil (A)	40¾	16.50	35.0
Buttes Gas & Oil (B)	17½	10.25	70.0
Beker Industries	65	15.87	65.0
Global Marine (A)	30¾	12.37	25.0
Global Marine (B)	31	16.00	100.0
Global Marine (C)	31	16.12	150.0
Pettibone	65⅛	12.37	20.00
Elsinor Corp.	71	14.00	25.0
Elsinor Finance	91¼	15.50	115.0
Total			$826.40

Arithmetic average: 44.33   13.98

Median: 38

Net default rate: (1.679) (1–.4433) + 50% of 13.98% coupon = 1.0046

Weighted average: $\dfrac{\Sigma(\text{EOM Price}) (\text{Amount})}{\Sigma(\text{Amount})} = \dfrac{37399.825}{826.40} = 45.25$

when a coupon payment is due). Using average historical default rates, we would expect this loss rate to occur on 1.53% of the par value of the portfolio. If we estimate the semiannual coupon to be between 4 and 7%, the net result is an annual loss in returns of between 96 and 101 basis points (0.96% to 1.01%).

100% − 41% = 59% loss of par value
0.59 × 153 = 90.3 basis point (BP) par value loss plus
0.04 × 153 = 6.1 BP coupon loss to
0.07 × 153 = 10.7 BP coupon loss

Total = 96.4 to 101.0 BP annual loss in returns

Again, this assumes that the investor purchased at par— a relevant assumption for some groups, for example, unit trust bond funds, but not relevant for others (investors in distressed firms). For example, the average price of our 70 bonds was 56.1% of par one year prior to default, indicating a 25.8% drop in price over the year prior to default. Purchasing at this date, at this price level, would have significantly reduced the basis point loss from defaults, compared to purchasing at par.

On a related subject, the average price of defaulting straight debt securities the month prior to bankruptcy or default was 50.1% of par, compared to 41% just after default. This indicates an 18.2% drop in value over the critical one month period prior to default. One might consider this result as the bond default announcement effect. Prior investigations into the announcement effect on common stock prices indicate that the drop in the equity price of bankrupt companies is substantially greater than for the debt, ranging from 25% (Altman, 1969) to 35 to 50% (Clark and Weinstein, 1983).

COMPARING DEFAULT RATES
WITH RETURNS

In our analysis for the portfolio management sections of this book (Chapters 8 and 9), it was found that holding a market basket (reconstituted at the end of each year) of straight, high yield bonds versus holding the equivalent of Shearson Lehman's Long-Term Government Bond Index, from December 31, 1977 to December 31, 1983, would have resulted in an annual compounded return spread of over 580 BPs in favor of the high yield bond portfolio. It should be noted that this premium or spread is sensitive to the starting and ending dates. For example, if the six year period was from March 1978 to March 1984, the spread was 490 BP. This premium to the high yield debt portfolio is net of defaults occurring over the period in the sample used. The 96 to 101 basis point default cost does indicate some risk in the high yield straight debt area, but the net returns are quite substantial, and will undoubtedly continue to attract investors to this market, if risk premiums stay at relatively high levels.

BOND AND INDUSTRY CHARACTERISTICS
OF DEFAULTING FIRMS

Prior Bond Ratings

Table 5-11 lists the original issue ratings of straight and convertible bonds which subsequently defaulted. While only 7.2% (9 of 125 issues) of the defaulting bonds were originally rated A or better, a total of 35 (28%) were originally rated investment grade. These "broken, fallen angels" demonstrate that firms can deteriorate from solid credits into bankruptcy or default at a later date. The largest per-

Table 5–11. Rating Distribution of Defaulting Issues at Various Points Prior to Default[a]

	AAA	AA	A	BBB	BB	B	CCC	CC	Total
Original rating									
Number	0	2	7	26	23	47	20	0	125
Percentage	0%	1.6%	5.6%	20.8%	18.4%	37.6%	16.0%	0%	100%
Rating one year prior									
Number	0	0	2	11	16	60	47	7	143
Percentage	0%	0%	1.4%	7.7%	11.2%	42.0%	32.9%	4.9%	100%
Rating six months prior									
Number	0	0	2	2	11	58	58	12	143
Percentage	0%	0%	1.4%	1.4%	7.7%	40.9%	40.3%	8.3%	100%

[a] Includes convertibles and straight debt issues. Excludes railroad issues. Ratings from *Standard & Poor's Bond Guide.*

131

centage (38%) of defaulting bonds were originally rated B.

While it is of some interest to examine the original rating of defaulting bonds, it is also quite relevant to assess the bond ratings as default approached. Rather than riding a bond all the way down, the portfolio manager can usually sell the security when its rating drops below some threshold level. In Table 5-11, we also examine defaulting bond ratings *12 months* and *six months* prior to reaching default status. The average rating is, as expected, lower than the original issue rating. We observed that 13 of 143 (9.1%) were rated investment grade one year prior to default and only 2.8% six months prior to default. Finally, only Manville's debt (two issues) was investment grade one month prior to filing. In summary, virtually all of the recent bond issue defaults were in the speculative or high yield (junk) categories just prior to default.

Industry Analysis

Tables 5-12 and 5-13 break out defaults by industry sector for 1970 to 1985. Railroad, oil and gas, retail and financial service companies had the largest proportional shares of the total (straight *and* convertible debt) dollar amounts defaulted. Including convertible defaults, the electronics/computer/communications sector had the largest *number* of firms defaulting.

In the straight debt default area, transportation companies were again well represented—including 9 major railroads. Since the number of railroads today is so few, the expected frequency of future defaults in this sector is low; the most recent major rail default was in 1977. Over the entire 16-year period though, the aggregate amount of publicly traded railroad debt defaulting accounted for over 27% of the total straight debt defaulted.

Table 5-12. Public Defaults by Industry Sector: 1970 to 1985 ($MM)

	Number of Companies	Straight Debt	Percent of Total Straight	Convertible Debt	Total in Default	Percent of Total
Industrial						
Retailers	14	$ 458.04	9.9%	$ 211.87	$ 669.91	10.2%
General manufacturing	18	420.55	9.1	152.84	573.39	8.7
Electrical/computer & communications	21	200.79	4.3	373.58	574.37	8.6
Oil & gas	18	695.44	15.0	405.95	1101.39	16.7
Real estate-construction, supplies	12	82.83	1.8	126.55	209.38	3.2
Miscellaneous industrials	17	570.30	12.3	166.88	737.18	11.2
Total industrial:	100	$2,427.95	52.4	$1,437.67	$3,865.62	58.6
Transportation						
Railroads	9	$1,260.22	27.2	$ 31.10	$1,291.32	19.6
Airlines/cargo	6	206.54	4.5	96.49	303.03	4.6
Sea lines	3	0.00	0.0	123.10	123.10	1.9
Trucks/motor carriers	3	48.31	1.0	9.75	58.06	0.9
Total transportation:	21	$1,515.07	32.7	$ 260.44	$1,775.51	27.0
Finance						
Financial service	10	$ 414.99	8.9	$ 164.04	$ 579.03	8.8
REITs	12	279.71	6.0	99.46	379.17	5.7
Total finance:	22	$ 694.70	15.0	$ 263.50	$ 958.20	14.5
Total defaults:[a]	143	$4,637.73	100.0%	$1,961.61	$6,599.33	100.0%

[a] Numbers may not add up due to rounding errors.

Table 5-13. Defaults by Industry Segment: 1970 to 1985 ($MM)

Segment	Straight Debt	Convertible Debt	Total Debt
Industrial			
Retailers			
Hardwick	$ 6.00	$ 0.00	$ 6.00
Wickes/Gambles Skogmo/Credit	263.04	28.10	291.14
Allied Supermarkets	0.00	19.50	19.50
Foodfair Corp.	41.30	0.00	41.30
United Merchants Mfg.	48.50	19.50	68.00
W. T. Grant	24.00	93.00	117.00
Daylin Corp.	53.30	0.00	53.30
Nat'l Bella Hess	0.00	3.70	3.70
Bohack Corp.	0.00	3.69	3.69
Interstate Stores	0.00	20.44	20.44
Parkview-GEM	0.00	2.60	2.60
Arden Mayfair	21.90	0.00	21.90
Arlan's Dept. Stores	0.00	15.50	15.50
Esgro Inc.	0.00	5.84	5.84
	458.04	211.87	669.91
General Manufacturing			
North American Car	46.82	0.00	46.82
Phoenix Steel	0.00	4.85	4.85
Revere Copper & Brass	0.00	41.30	41.30
Johns Manville Corp.	175.00	0.00	175.00
AM Int'l	37.00	11.10	48.10
Std. Packaging/Saxon	11.10	32.70	43.80

134

Morton Shoes	11.50	0.00	11.50
Duplan Corp.	0.00	21.20	21.20
Gray Mfg.	0.00	2.38	2.38
Omega-Alpha Corp.	25.00	0.00	25.00
Lyntex	0.00	13.80	13.80
Elcor Chemical	0.00	12.40	12.40
Roberts Co.	5.03	0.00	5.03
Mego Int'l	14.10	0.00	14.10
Lionel	15.00	0.00	15.00
Sharon Steel	60.00	0.00	60.00
Macrodyne Industries	0.00	13.21	13.21
Pettibone Corp.	20.00	0.00	20.00
	420.55	152.94	573.49
Computers/Electronics/Communications			
Storage Tech/Documation	131.00	83.00	214.00
Anacomp	0.00	50.00	50.00
Altec Corp.	7.84	2.71	10.55
Pioneer Texas (DPA)	0.00	4.50	4.50
Amer. Communications	20.00	0.00	20.00
Combustion Equipment	16.20	13.30	29.50
Dasa	0.00	2.55	2.55
Inforex	20.00	0.00	20.00
Wyly Corp.	0.00	19.60	19.60
Optical Scanning	0.00	5.42	5.42
Nat'l Telephone	0.00	2.50	2.50
Electro Space	0.00	9.99	9.99
Boothe Computers	0.00	17.90	17.90
Harvard Ind.	5.75	3.00	8.75

Table 5-13. Defaults by Industry Segment: 1970 to 1985 ($MM) (Continued)

Segment	Straight Debt	Convertible Debt	Total Debt
Waltham Ind.	0.00	8.00	8.00
Viatron Computer	0.00	25.00	25.00
Computer Application	0.00	18.60	18.60
Fairfield Technology	0.00	2.00	2.00
Visual Electronics	0.00	1.71	1.71
Farrington Mfg.	0.00	3.80	3.80
Oak Industries	0.00	100.00	100.00
	200.79	373.58	574.37
Oil and Gas			
Kenai Corp.	27.50	0.00	27.50
TransCont. Energy	5.44	0.00	5.44
Commonwealth Oil ('84 & '78)	0.00	57.90	57.90
Tomlinson Oil	0.00	15.65	15.65
Texas General Resources	30.00	0.00	30.00
Page Petroleum	0.00	25.00	25.00
Anglo Energy	17.50	0.00	17.50
Peninsula Resources ('83 & '85)	0.00	30.00	30.00
MGF Oil	75.00	0.00	75.00
Marion Corp.	0.00	20.00	20.00
Amarex	30.00	0.00	30.00
Nucorp Energy	0.00	110.00	110.00
King Resources	0.00	24.40	24.40

Buttes Gas and Oil	105.00	0.00	105.00
American Quasar Petroleum	65.00	0.00	65.00
Oxoco Inc.	65.00	0.00	65.00
Global Marine	275.00	123.00	398.00
	695.44	405.95	1101.39
Real Estate: construction, development, supplies, miscellaneous			
Land Resources	0.00	16.30	16.30
Rusco Ind.	0.00	6.19	6.19
Penn-Dixie Inc.	0.00	9.00	9.00
Frigitemp	0.00	5.00	5.00
Permaneer Corp.	0.00	13.17	13.17
GAC Prop. Credit	79.30	0.00	79.30
Hallcraft Homes	0.00	15.00	15.00
Wolf Corp.	3.53	3.53	3.53
U.S. Financial Serv.	0.00	35.00	35.00
DCA Development	0.00	3.80	3.80
Shelter Resources	0.00	11.00	11.00
Punta Gorda Isles	0.00	12.09	12.09
	82.83	126.55	209.38
Miscellaneous Industrial			
Pizzatime Theater	0.00	50.00	50.00
Allied Artists	0.00	3.10	3.10
Charter Co.	106.10	0.00	106.10
Wilson Foods	45.70	0.00	45.70
Grolier Inc.	30.00	22.50	52.50
Sanitas Services	0.00	8.20	8.20
Career Academy	0.00	1.32	1.32

Table 5-13. Defaults by Industry Segment: 1970 to 1985 ($MM) (Continued)

Segment	Straight Debt	Convertible Debt	Total Debt
Westgate-Calif.	7.60	16.40	24.00
Sherwood Diversified/Leasing	0.00	12.90	12.90
FAS Int'l	0.00	16.34	16.34
Great Mark Western Pkg.	0.00	2.50	2.50
Hunt International Resources	31.40	0.00	31.40
Beker Industries	65.00	0.00	65.00
Elsinore Corporation/Finance	140.00	0.00	140.00
Castle and Cooke	100.00	19.42	119.42
Brock Hotel	44.50	0.00	44.50
Delmed Inc.	0.00	14.20	14.20
	570.30	166.88	737.18
Total Industrial:	$2,427.95	$1,437.77	$3,865.62
Finance/Real Estate			
REITs			
Regency Investors	$ 0.00	$ 17.20	$ 17.20
South Atlantic Trust	16.90	0.00	16.90
Chase Mhtn. Mtge.	77.60	30.90	108.50
Tri South Mtge.	24.30	12.40	36.70
First Mtge. Inv.	28.80	0.00	28.80
Guardian Mtge. Inv.	33.00	0.21	33.21
Great Am. Mtge. & Trust	50.00	0.00	50.00

Justice Mtge.	19.60	0.00	19.60
Treco	4.51	0.00	4.51
Colwell Mtge. & Trust	25.00	0.00	25.00
Continental Mtge.	0.00	36.00	36.00
Fidelity Mtge. Inv.	0.00	2.75	2.75
	279.71	99.46	379.17
Financial Services/Leasing			
Baldwin-United	46.20	0.00	46.20
California Life Fin.	20.00	0.00	20.00
Emons	27.30	0.00	27.30
Itel	184.60	0.00	184.60
FSC Inc.	7.00	2.61	9.61
American Reserve	0.00	7.60	7.60
Continental Investors	37.20	1.67	38.87
Investors Funding	49.49	90.76	140.25
Equity Funding of Am.	22.00	61.40	83.40
Mission Insurance Group	21.20	0.00	21.20
	414.99	164.04	579.03
Total Financial	$ 694.70	$ 263.50	$ 958.20
Transportation			
Railroads (Majors)			
Chicago, Milw. & St. P. RR ('77 & '70)	$ 146.37	$ 31.10	$ 177.47
Chicago, RI & Pac. RR	47.50	0.00	47.50
Ann Arbor Mich. RR	5.17	0.00	5.17
Erie RR	187.50	0.00	187.50
Reading RR	82.00	0.00	82.00
Boston Maine RR	46.30	0.00	46.30

Table 5-13. Defaults by Industry Segment: 1970 to 1985 ($MM) (Continued)

Segment	Straight Debt	Convertible Debt	Total Debt
Cleveland C&C & St. L. RR	76.50	0.00	76.50
Lehigh Valley RR	50.70	0.00	50.70
Penn Central RR	618.18	0.00	618.18
	1,260.22	31.10	1,291.32
Airlines/Air Cargo			
Texas Int'l/Continental Airlines	47.84	47.29	95.13
Flight Transportation	25.00	0.00	25.00
Braniff Airlines	133.70	0.00	133.70
Mohawk Airlines	0.00	8.00	8.00
Ozark Airlines	0.00	22.20	22.20
Airlift Int'l	0.00	19.00	19.00
	206.54	96.49	303.03
Auto/Motor Carrier			
Telecom Corp.	25.00	0.00	25.00
Spector Inc.	0.00	3.00	3.00
White Motor	23.31	6.75	30.06
	48.31	9.75	58.06
Ocean Carriers			
Sea Train Lines	0.00	50.00	50.00
American Export	0.00	60.00	60.00
Tacoma Boatbuilding	0.00	13.10	13.10
	0.00	123.10	123.10
Total Transportation:	$1,515.07	$ 260.44	$1,775.51
Total defaults:	$4,637.72	$1,961.71	$6,599.43

Oil and gas companies represented 16.7% of all (straight and convertible) defaults at the end of 1985, while retailers and financial services companies represented 10.2 and 8.8% of defaulted debt, respectively. The precipitous drop in oil prices in 1985 critically affected that industry, causing its portion of total defaults to increase dramatically from just 8.6% at the end of 1984.

Finance company defaults, particularly the real estate investment trusts (REITs) in the mid-1970s, were numerous. While the number of future REIT defaults is not likely to be high due to a much diminished pool to draw from, the dynamic and increasingly competitive nature of the finance industry should portend an increased number of bankruptcies and perhaps bond defaults. This latter forecast must be tempered, because few large financial institutions presently tap the public debt markets, and rely instead on short-term paper, public agency borrowing, and deposits. In addition, deregulation is taking its toll of finance-related firms and transport companies, including airlines. Over time, however, the most vulnerable sectors change and it is difficult to project these trends into the future.

CORPORATE DEBT DEFAULTS AND BUSINESS FAILURES

The business failure rate, published by Dun & Bradstreet, and bankruptcy filing experience of firms in the United States reached record postdepression levels in 1983 (see Table 5-14). Aggregate GNP data show that 1982 marked the bottom of the most recent recession, a fact that is reflected in our default data. It is difficult, however, to establish a clear connection between aggregate business failure rates in the United States and corporate default rates. In some years, the directional change from the prior year is fairly consistent

Table 5-14. Bankruptcy and Business Failure Statistics in the United States: 1974 to 1985

Year	Number of Business Bankruptcy Filings	Yearly Change	Business Failures	Yearly Change	Business Failure Rate[a]	Yearly Change
1985	66,651	7%	57,067[b]	10%[b]	114	7%
1984	62,170	(11)	52,078[b]	66[b]	107	(3)
1983	69,818	24	31,334	26	110	24
1982	56,423	19	24,908	46	89	46
1981	47,414	30	17,041	45	61	45
1980	36,513	24	11,742	55	42	50
1979	29,500	(3)	7,564	14	28	17
1978	30,528	(5)	6,619	(16)	24	(14)
1977	32,189	(9)	7,919	(18)	28	(20)
1976	35,201	17	9,628	(16)	35	(19)
1975	30,130	45	11,432	15	43	13
1974	20,747	19	9,915	6	38	6

Source: Administrative Office of Bankruptcy Courts, Division of Bankruptcy Statistics; Fiscal year ends June and, Dun & Bradstreet's (NJ), Business Failure Statistics, annually.

[a] Dun & Bradstreet changed its reporting system in 1984 and no longer reports the failure rate (failures per 10,000 listed companies); 1984 to 85 statistics estimated by E. Altman.

[b] The Dun & Bradstreet data base changed significantly in 1984 and 1985 when over 50,000 business failures were counted.

between these two seemingly related series. For example, in 1982, the business failure rate and number of bankruptcies in the United States rose significantly while the total and especially the low-rated corporate default rate also increased dramatically. Other recent, "consistent" years were: 1975 (up), 1976 (down), 1978 (down), 1980 (up), and 1984 (down). In contrast, 1977, 1979, 1981, 1983, and 1985 do not show this consistent pattern. Therefore, the failure rate in any one year is not especially meaningful for estimating defaults of publicly held company debt. At the same time, it appears that the changing, less regulated structure of the United States economy portends relatively high business failure numbers, not necessarily rates, in the future. Bond defaults, however, should continue to fluctuate more widely.

CONCLUDING COMMENTS

We have documented the default rate experience of high yield corporate debt, in particular, the experience over the last decade and a half. On the one hand, we might conclude that a default rate that can be expected to average over 1.50% per year depicts a somewhat risky scenario. A portfolio with a buy-and-hold strategy can expect its capital base to deteriorate fairly rapidly, especially if coupon income is paid out to investors. On the other hand, returns on low-quality debt portfolios have been very impressive, even after defaults.

For more cautious investors, hedging and diversification strategies are possible to reduce both the risks and returns on such portfolios. Another strategy might be to search the high yield universe for the more acceptable risk-return relationships and then to diversify within this "quality-junk" segment of the high yield market. Either way, reductions in losses due to defaults should result. We will explore these risk and return tradeoffs in more depth in Chapters 8 and 9.

6

Assessing Credit Quality and Default Risks

IMPORTANCE OF CREDIT QUALITY

Successful investing in high yield bonds requires that investors accurately assess the credit quality of the individual issuing firms as well as the overall credit exposure in their portfolio. Credit research techniques should be designed to significantly reduce the probability of large (downward) variations from expected returns due to deterioration in the operating and financial characteristics of the issuing firms. All debt securities are subject to overall interest rate or market risk that causes fluctuations in the market value of a portfolio. But high yield bonds are more sensitive to company specific news, as the issues usually operate closer to levels of financial distress and default than do their investment grade counterparts. In a sense, junk bond holders have a greater chance of becoming equity owners in the firms they invest in (as a result of reorganizations or restructurings), thereby causing increased concern and reaction to changes in issuer performance. Some analysts, in effect, view junk bonds as a type of equity security. These reactions can cause substantial shifts in the market value of an issuer's debt and will lead to greater variability in the return over time if the investor is not careful. How an investor assesses the total credit picture of a firm, we feel, is an important element in the long run success of an investment program. While we advocate prudency and thoughtful investing in all securities, high yield bonds require even greater caution.

CREDIT EVALUATION TECHNIQUES

Traditional financial statement analysis is basically a univariate approach whereby individual measures of firm performance, primarily ratios, are compared with other firms in the same sector or bond rating, and also examined over time to assess trends. Performance categories such as liquidity, profitability, cash flow, leverage, solvency, and asset turnover are typical concerns of most analyses. See Frisdon and Marocco, in Altman (1986a) for a discussion on ratios and financial statement analysis.

While a pervasive tool among credit practitioners, traditional ratio analysis suffers from potential problems in ambiguity, subjectivity, and misleading indicators. Essentially, there is no "bottom line" as to firm performance and risk attributes. Hence, the final determination is a subjective product of the individual analyzing the ratios. Since our goal is to assess the credit quality of hundreds of firms in the high yield market and to compare aggregate measures with investment grade securities over time, we need an objective approach which is capable of summarizing a number of disparate operating and financial characteristics into a single, unambiguous measure.

The Zeta™ Credit Evaluation Model

We chose Zeta™ credit evaluation scores, acquired from Zeta Services, Inc., (Hoboken, NJ) to assess credit quality in our high yield firm universe. Zeta was developed by Altman, Haldeman, and Narayanan (1977) to identify the bankruptcy risk of industrial corporations. Building on earlier bankruptcy classification works, Zeta combines traditional financial measures with a multivariate technique known as discriminant analysis so as to lead to an overall "credit-score" for each of the firms being examined. This model is of the form:

$$\text{Zeta} = a_0 + a_1 X_1 + a_2 X_2 + a_3 X_3 \ldots a_n X_n$$

where Zeta = overall credit score
$X_1 \ldots X_n$ = Explanatory variables (ratios and market measures)
$a_0 \ldots a_n$ = Weightings or coefficients

The model was derived from a comparison of over 100 industrial firms. Of those firms approximately half filed for bankruptcy reorganization while the other half represented a healthy, control group of firms. The final Zeta model included seven financial measures. Each of the seven was based on data adjusted for the latest accounting financial statement treatments and those thought likely to be required in the years subsequent to Zeta's construction, for example, the Financial Accounting Standards Board requirements on lease capitalization.

Zeta Score Variables

X_1 = Profitability—earnings before interest and taxes (EBIT)/total assets
X_2 = Stability of earnings measure—standard error of estimate of EBIT/TA (normalized) for 10 years
X_3 = Debt service capabilities—EBIT/interest charges
X_4 = Cumulative profitability—retained earnings/total assets

$X_5 =$ Liquidity measure—current assets/current liabilities
$X_6 =$ Capitalization levels over time—5 year average market value of equity/total capitalization
$X_7 =$ Size—total tangible assets, normalized

The model was extremely accurate in assigning firms from the original sample of bankrupt and nonbankrupt companies. The accuracy levels for the bankrupt group were from 96% one annual statement prior to bankruptcy to about 70% five annual statements prior. Even more important, the model has proven to be extremely accurate in subsequent tests. Table 6-1 lists Zeta scores for 64 recent bankrupt firms with 61 (95%) correctly identified (based on a negative Zeta score at one financial statement prior) and 90, 78, 67, and 63% accuracy up to five annual statements prior.

The lower the firm's Zeta score, the more "in-distress" the model indicates. Negative Zetas do not indicate default or bankruptcy with certainty but the lower the score, the greater the similarity between that particular firm and those that have gone bankrupt in the past. The average Zeta score for the past bankrupts was about -4.0 in the original sample and -5.0 for those filing subsequent to the model's construction (Table 6-1).

Zetas, Defaults, and Bond Rating Analysis

The association between bankruptcy prediction and defaults is obvious. We will utilize Zeta scores as our credit evaluation model both in the assessment of the trend in credit quality of new issuers in the high yield debt market and in portfolio construction strategies. First, it is instructive to examine the Zeta score equivalents for the different categories of bonds rated by Standard & Poor's and Moody's. We would expect that the higher the average Zeta score, the higher the firm's credit quality and also its bond rating. That is exactly what we observe in Table 6-2 and Exhibit 6-1.

Note that the average single-A company's Zeta score for both rating agencies was about 5.6 in 1985, up only slightly from the 5.3 level in 1978. Indeed, all ratings show a rather flat trend for this period indicating that rating agency credit standards have remained remarkably unchanged over time. We will observe a somewhat different trend for new high yield bond issuers in the next section. The only exception to this flat trend is the rise in average Zeta scores for the lower rating categories (CCC and B) in the 1979—1981 period and the subsequent deterioration for these categories in the more recent 1982–1985 period. Perhaps this reflects the fallen-angel effect whereby these once investment-grade companies began to deteriorate in the early 1980s but not yet to the point of existing very low-rated companies. Then, despite the subsequent economic expansion, many of these firms continued to deteriorate.

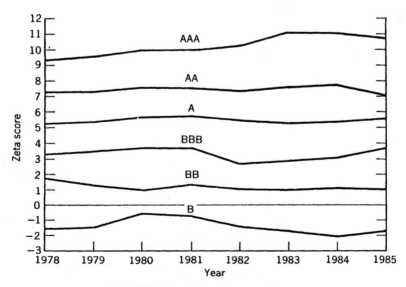

Exhibit 6-1 Zeta score vs. time.

Table 6-1. Companies Which Have Failed Since ZETA Was Developed: 1977 to 1982

Company	Date Bankrupt	Final Statement Date	At Final Statement Date	ZETA Scores				Number of Months with Negative Score Prior to Failure
				Final Statement Date −1	Final Statement Date −2	Final Statement Date −3	Final Statement Date −4	
AM International	4/14/82	7/81	−4.60	−0.18	0.35	1.01	0.32	20
Acme Hamilton Mfg.	2/28/78	10/76	−5.54	−4.40	−4.25	−4.00	−4.12	124
Advent	3/17/81	3/80	−6.10	−4.22	−1.41	—	—	36
Alan Wood Steel	6/10/77	12/76	−4.92	−3.18	−0.31	−0.84	−1.33	89
Allied Artists	4/05/79	3/78	−7.07	−8.18	−7.14	−2.29	−1.40	120
Allied Supermarkets	11/06/78	6/78	−6.11	−5.28	−4.59	−2.92	−2.41	88
Apeco Corp.	10/19/77	11/76	−8.29	−1.53	−2.16	0.94	4.67	35
Arctic Enterprises	2/17/81	3/80	−4.12	−2.06	−0.78	0.26	0.54	35
Auto Train Corp.	9/80	12/79	−9.30	−8.42	−5.76	—	—	33
Barclay Inds. Inc.	6/81	7/80	−10.47	−4.80	−3.78	−2.83	−0.17	59
Bobbie Brooks	1/17/82	4/81	−1.98	−1.69	−0.29	−0.97	−3.03	103
Braniff Airlines	5/13/82	12/80	−3.40	−2.18	1.21	1.02	0.63	28
B. Brody Seating	2/04/80	8/79	−4.87	−3.02	−1.15	−0.41	−1.32	53
Capehart Corp.	2/16/79	3/78	−11.34	−6.54	—	—	—	24
Commonwealth Oil	3/03/78	12/76	−2.57	−1.72	0.26	0.63	1.12	26
Cooper Jarrett	12/28/81	12/80	−8.56	−6.93	−5.18	−4.04	−3.98	120
Eagle Clothes	11/01/77	12/75	−2.89	−2.38	−2.30	−1.83	−1.18	70
Ernst, E.C.	12/04/78	3/78	−4.49	0.78	2.00	1.81	2.04	8
FDI Inc.	12/01/78	4/77	−5.75	−5.93	−5.06	−0.58	−0.45	79
Filigree Foods	4/02/76	7/74	−3.89	−3.97	−3.80	−4.87	−5.62	68
First Hartford	2/23/81	4/79	−10.00	−7.30	−7.67	−5.45	−5.42	123
Food Fair Inc.	10/03/78	7/77	−0.61	−0.68	−1.01	0.52	0.62	38
Frigitemps	3/24/78	12/76	−1.65	−1.08	—	—	—	27
GRT Corp.	7/14/79	3/78	−3.46	−1.62	−2.92	—	—	39

Garcia Corp.	8/08/78	7/77	- 4.69	-2.49	0.61	—	—	24
Garland Corp.	4/29/80	10/79	- 1.85	-0.61	-0.04	2.54	0.70	30
General Recreation	12/21/78	12/77	-14.41	-6.79	-4.39	-0.67	—	48
Goldblatt Bros.	6/16/81	1/80	- 2.35	-1.71	-0.59	0.36	0.46	41
Good, L. S. & Co.	5/27/80	1/79	- 2.75	-2.17	-1.63	-1.37	-1.31	64
Inforex	10/79	12/78	- 3.69	-4.22	-3.66	-4.43	—	46
Itel	1/19/81	12/79	6.62	-1.79	-1.88	-1.15	-1.68	85
Keydata Corp.	11/31/80	7/80	-15.79	-9.55	-8.44	-7.25	-7.17	64
Lionel	2/82	12/80	- 1.61	-1.91	-2.19	-1.23	-1.70	121
Lynnwear Corp.	2/81	11/79	5.46	-2.05	-2.10	-1.80	-0.94	98
Mansfield Tire	10/79	12/78	8.20	1.09	1.31	0.90	0.84	22
Mays, T. W. Inc.	1/26/82	7/81	- 2.03	-1.04	0.44	0.40	-0.74	78
McLouth Steel	12/08/81	12/80	2.17	0.32	0.34	0.45	2.29	11
Metropolitan Greetings	1/18/79	12/77	5.94	-3.89	-3.63	-2.45	—	49
Morton Shoe Cos.	1/01/82	6/81	5.05	-2.72	-1.32	-2.05	-2.26	137
National Shoes	12/12/80	1/79	2.56	-1.05	-0.41	—	—	46
Neisner Bros. Inc.	12/77	1/77	- 2.84	-3.02	-1.81	-0.98	-1.07	58
Nelly Don Inc.	11/29/78	11/77	-16.73	-7.11	-4.28	-3.40	-1.70	72
Novo Corp.	9/78	12/76	5.03	-4.66	-3.36	-3.07	-3.23	128
Pacific Far East	1/02/78	12/76	3.52	-3.95	-4.28	-4.74	-2.41	72
Pathcom	11/30/81	12/80	-29.56	—	—	—	—	11
Penn Dixie Inds.	4/07/80	12/78	- 2.88	-3.54	-1.71	-1.28	0.15	51
Piedmont Inds.	2/22/79	5/78	- 1.90	-1.38	—	—	—	21
Red Ball Express (Telecom Score)	4/26/82	12/80	2.75	-0.58	-0.62	-0.78	-2.46	94
Richton International	3/18/80	4/79	0.15	1.08	0.49	0.25	-0.59	0[a]
Sambo's Restaurants	11/82	12/80	3.51	-4.28	-0.54	1.10	1.32	35
Saxon Inds.	4/15/82	12/80	0.27	-0.06	0.14	-0.34	-0.50	0[a]
Seatrain Lines	2/11/81	6/80	- 2.41	-2.69	-2.58	-2.77	-3.27	115
Shulman Trans. Ent.	8/21/78	12/77	7.31	-4.29	-2.58	—	—	32
Sitkin Smlt & Ref.	3/13/78	6/77	4.07	-3.12	-1.24	-1.52	-0.17	68

Source: ZETA Services, Inc., Hoboken, NJ. Chart compiled by R. Haldeman for conference in Bankruptcy, "Reorganization Under Chapter 11: Investor/Lender Viewpoint," New York, May 14, 1982.
[a] Errors in prediction

Table 6-1. Companies Which Have Failed Since ZETA Was Developed: 1977 to 1982 (Continued)

Company	Date Bankrupt	Final Statement Date	ZETA Scores At Final Statement Date	Final Statement Date −1	Final Statement Date −2	Final Statement Date −3	Final Statement Date −4	Number of Months with Negative Score Prior to Failure
Solomon, Sam Inc.	8/29/80	1/79	− 2.03	2.09	—	—	—	31
Stelber Industries	3/10/76	6/73	− 5.97	−2.40	−2.21	−2.93	−3.94	80
Stevcoknit Inc.	11/81	1/81	− 2.47	−2.45	−0.07	0.01	0.70	34
Tenna Corp.	6/25/81	1/79	− 0.70	−1.52	1.87	2.21	3.36	41
United Merch & Mfg.	7/12/77	6/76	− 0.38	0.24	1.72	3.23	3.04	12
Universal Cont'r	3/22/78	11/76	− 5.03	−5.32	−4.02	−2.96	−2.26	111
West Chem Prods.	2/29/79	11/78	− 0.31	0.35	5.70	5.98	5.44	3[a]
White Motor Corp.	9/04/80	12/79	− 1.41	−1.95	−1.80	−1.85	−2.39	116
Wickes Cos.	4/25/82	1/81	− 0.92	0.39	0.48	0.77	0.91	15
Wilson Freight Co.	7/80	12/79	− 3.87	—	—	—	—	7
Average Score			− 5.04	−2.93	−1.81	−1.10	−0.84	
Number of firms correctly classified			61	56	45	35	31	
Number of firms incorrectly classified			3	6	13	17	18	
Total number of firms			64	62	58	52	49	
Percent correct			95	90	78	67	63	
Percent incorrect			5	10	22	33	37	
Average number of months of lead time								57

Source: ZETA Services, Inc., Hoboken, NJ. Chart compiled by R. Haldeman for conference in Bankruptcy, "Reorganization Under Chapter 11: Investor/Lender Viewpoint," New York, May 14, 1982.
[a] Errors in prediction

Table 6-2. Average Zeta Scores By Rating Agency and By Rating Category (Senior Debt Bond Rating—Zeta Scores)

	1978	1979	1980	1981	1982	1983	1984	1985
Standard & Poor's								
AAA	9.33	9.49	10.00	10.03	10.34	11.17	11.01	10.79
AA	7.30	7.32	7.48	7.58	7.29	7.58	7.71	7.16
A	5.29	5.30	5.62	5.65	5.39	5.20	5.32	5.57
BBB	3.31	3.51	3.75	3.61	2.71	2.81	3.15	3.67
BB	1.73	1.20	1.03	1.38	1.09	1.06	1.10	1.09
B	−1.60	−1.42	−0.52	−0.79	−1.43	−1.74	−2.06	−1.64
CCC	−5.35	−4.29	−2.45	−2.59	−4.23	−4.46	−4.05	−2.16
Moody's								
Aaa	9.16	9.34	9.80	9.87	10.54	10.99	10.95	11.15
Aa	7.49	7.56	7.48	7.61	7.57	7.83	7.79	7.55
A	5.28	5.23	5.62	5.60	5.42	5.35	5.56	5.66
Baa	2.93	3.08	3.44	3.43	2.88	3.07	3.11	3.49
Ba	1.06	0.89	0.87	1.00	1.29	0.79	1.20	0.67
B	−2.56	−1.80	−0.24	−0.69	−1.62	−2.18	−2.53	−1.20
Caa	−5.50	−5.45	−6.08	−3.69	−4.97	−4.51	−4.04	−6.20

Source: Zeta Services, Inc., Hoboken, NJ, 1986

Credit Quality of Individual Issuers

We investigated credit quality and risk identification from several dimensions. The primary assessment tool used was the Zeta credit risk model. We also examined the trends of numerous traditional ratio measures of performance but found it difficult to summarize credit quality from a large number of sometimes disparate results. Hence, the unambiguous, composite statistic of Zeta was utilized to assess:

1. The trend in Zeta of new issuer, high yield straight debt securities over time, relative to the absolute levels and trends of existing bonds in the different bond rating categories.

2. The default prediction qualities of Zeta with particular emphasis on the securities in the Morgan Stanley data base— the data base we used to assess portfolio attributes of high yield debt securities in Chapters 8 and 9.

New Issuer Credit Quality and Default Risk Assessment: 1978-1984

Between 1978 and 1984, new issuer, high yield securities appear to have experienced an upward (better quality) trend (with the exception of 1983). Table 6-3 lists the median and average Zeta scores of new issuer firms. In 1978, the central tendency of new issuer scores was roughly equivalent or slightly above the average S&P single-B rated debt. Note that the high yield new issuer's score increased from a -1.05 median in 1978 to -0.65 in 1980. But we observed that the trend was also favorable for all single-B rated debt in that three-year period. Indeed, the median or average high yield new issuer score was just about the same (-0.65) as all S&P single-B rated debt (-0.52) in 1980.

The divergence between the trend in new issuer, high yield debt and the entire debt market started to take place in

1981. Exhibit 6-2 clearly illustrates these differences. The Zeta trend in *new issuer* debt rated BB or B continued to improve in the 1981 to 1984 period (except 1983), especially the median score, while the overall BB/B market deteriorated in the face of the recession. This deterioration has continued in the most recent expansionary years. No doubt, a number of deteriorating higher grade securities, the so-called fallen angels, helped to contribute to this decline. The trend in investment grade debt rated BBB and A was only slightly negative over this most recent period and was essentially unchanged from 1978 to 1984.

While the overall credit profile of new, high yield debt issuers is still in the risky zone, around a Zeta of zero, we observed an overall improvement in this group both in absolute and relative terms. This does not mean that the credit analyst or risk arbitrageur can relax, because the distribution of scores is quite wide with several new issues fairly

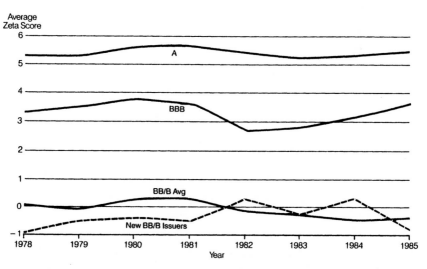

Exhibit 6-2 Zeta scores: new vs. existing issuers rated BB/B by S&P.

deep in the negative Zeta zone [7 of 46 (15%) had Zetas −3.0 or below in 1983 and 7 of 53 (13%) in 1984]. Still, if one had to assess the average quality of the new issue, high yield marketplace, the conclusion would be a slight improvement over the 1978 to 1984 period.

Credit Quality and Returns—1985

In 1985, high yield issues were on average smaller, less creditworthy by quantitative criteria, and more likely to be unrated than in 1984. Despite that trend, high yield bond funds outperformed most other fixed income categories for the year (see Chapter 4).

The 1985 high yield new issuance and performance statistics indicate that thorough credit analysis, which is always important, became even more crucial. The investor could not simply "buy the market," confident that the incremental yield on low-rated bonds would overwhelm default rates.

In 1985, for the first time since the development of a major primary high yield debt market, the average size of new issues declined. While new issue volume was essentially flat compared to 1984 at just under $15 billion, the number of financings rose by about 50%, and the number of very large issues dropped. As a result, average issue size fell to $78.0 million, below both 1984's $120.6 million and 1983's $86.2 million. Average issue size dropped partly because the number of very large financings declined. To the extent that the trend also reflected offerings by smaller companies, though, investors need to reaffirm their resolve

Much of this material comes from work we did for Morgan Stanley and reported in Fridson, Martin S., "Credit Trends and Returns—1985," *High Performance*, March 1986, Morgan Stanley & Co., Incorporated, pp. 2–9.

to maintain their credit standards. Smallness, per se, does not imply greater risk, but some of its frequent concomitants do—undiversified product lines, vulnerability to prolonged price wars against deeper-pocketed competitors, and lack of strong management below the most senior levels. Owing to such causes, firm size has predictive value in measuring default risk and is consequently one of the variables in our Zeta model.

The proliferation of smaller deals does not in itself demonstrate dilution of new issue quality, but in conjunction with certain other trends, raises justifiable concern. For instance, Table 2-5, in Chapter 2, reveals a marked shift in the distribution of new issues by rating category. In dollar terms, BB issues fell from 31.4% of total new issuance in 1984 to 13.9% in 1985, while nonrated issues jumped from 6.7% to 26.3% of the total. Even more striking were the figures for number of issues, with nonrated deals rising from 15.3% to 33.5% of the total. There are a number of legitimate reasons why an issuer declines to seek a rating, particularly for a small issue. For the investor however, the absence of ratings eliminates two or more independent assessments of the issuer's quality. The investor may be able to rank the borrower among its industry peers and price it on the basis of public information, but must consider that no impartial observer has examined the nonpublic data to which the rating agencies would ordinarily be privy.

Not only did smaller and nonrated issues become more prevalent in 1985, but quantitative indications show that credit risk deteriorated. Both median and average Zeta scores of new high yield issues declined following an upturn in 1984 (Table 6-3). Unfortunately, Zeta scores were available on a smaller portion of the new issues than in any year since 1978. This reflects substantial issuance by companies outside Zeta's data base, which includes all industrial compa-

Table 6-3. High Yield New Issuer Zeta Scores: 1978 to 1985[a]

Year	Number of New Issues	Number of Companies with Zeta Scores	Median Zeta	Average Zeta
1985	188	46	− 0.24	− 0.86
1984	124	53	0.35	0.31
1983	86	46	− 0.15	− 0.30
1982	48	20	0.30	0.29
1981	32	15	− 0.03	− 0.52
1980	43	24	− 0.65	− 0.40
1979	45	33	− 0.84	− 0.54
1978	52	27	− 1.05	− 0.96

[a] Straight debt only. Does not include convertible or exchange offers.

nies listed on the New York and American stock exchanges, plus selected over-the-counter companies. As with size, merely being unlisted or obscure does not necessarily imply poor credit quality. Fixed income investors often cannot tap equity research on such companies, however. Furthermore, private companies account for much of the 1985 crop of non-Zeta-scored issues. For this group, investors cannot follow a quoted stock price, which is perhaps the short-term credit barometer most widely used by high yield portfolio managers. Furthermore, companies with no public shares sometimes feel obliged to offer no more information to bondholders than the bare minimum prescribed by the Securities and Exchange Commission. As a final point on Zeta, Table 6-2 shows that the 1985 decline in scores of new issuers did not cause the general deterioration of the combined average of the BB and B issuer (old and new) categories, which actually turned up slightly in 1985. After running above the outstanding and newly issued BB and B average from 1982 to 1984, the new issue mean fell below it in 1985.

If new issue credit quality is indeed trending lower, we

might expect default rates to rise in consequence in the coming years. Actually, it is too soon for the 1985 vintage to show spoilage; the upturn in default rates in 1985 may therefore indicate that the quality dilution that became apparent in the 1985 data has been developing for some time. The 1.68% default rate (Chapter 5), up from 0.83% in 1984, however, is far short of a record.

It is possible to exaggerate the significance of defaults in the total returns of a high yield bond portfolio because the associated losses may be offset by gains on upgradings that result from takeovers by much larger, high grade companies or simply from improved finances. In practice, however, portfolio managers' clients and investment committees are not indifferent to a 30 basis point loss offset by three (or four) 10 basis point gains, making default avoidance tactics essential.

Nonetheless, default statistics should help emphasize our theme of the need for close scrutiny of high yield issuers. This is particularly so in view of the surge of exchange offers by distressed companies during 1985, not all of which will work out successfully (e.g., LTV Corp.). Incidentally, the 1985 Zeta score for LTV Corporation was a deeply distressed -4.

These unsettling trends did not mar the low-rated sector's performance in 1985. High yield mutual funds outperformed all other categories except their closest kinsmen, the triple-B funds. Actually, portfolios of very long term bonds (government or corporate) performed best in 1985. This vitality confounded those who pronounced the high yield market dead following its comparatively low return in 1984. Over the 3- and 10-year periods, moreover, high yield debt funds led the field (see Chapters 2 and 4 for details). To date, high yield managers have validated the notion that the sector can produce superior returns over extended periods, notwithstanding episodes of high default.

Some observers wonder, though, whether the train is about to derail, owing to the hazards pointed out earlier. Sensationalizing journalists are not alone in raising the question; many investment professionals also express concern about credit quality. We share some of those concerns and believe that in order to continue to achieve high performance in low-rated bonds, investors will have to be discriminating. Fridson (1986) notes that he "would not be surprised to see a two-tier market emerge if credit problems multiply." Companies that began with sound finances and have not subsequently overextended their debt obligations will continue to be attractive vehicles for long-term investors who adequately diversify. The lower class of issuers, however, will drag down the performance of portfolio managers who merely go through the motions of credit analysis.

The good news for those who are willing to put their minds to the task is that analyzing high yield credits does not involve secrets that have been revealed to only few persons. Certainly, investors can periodically uncover bargains by mining their industry contacts and poring over less widely read trade journals. However, there is no substitute for thorough credit screening and analysis techniques. For instance, in 1985 our Zeta model successfully anticipated all of the defaults for which scores were available. Of the 17 issues (including convertibles) that defaulted in 1985, Zeta scores were available on 13. In all 13 cases, Zeta scores were below zero (the cutoff between healthy and distressed firms) one year before default, with scores averaging − 5.14 at that point. Two years before default all but two companies were already below zero, with the − 2.44 average signaling substantial distress. See Table 6-4 for these results.

If this purely quantitative technique, using information that is already broadly disseminated (i.e., reported financial data), can do that well, then an institution with the added

Table 6-4. Zeta Scores for 1985 Defaults

	Zeta Score			
	1 Year Prior		2 Years Prior	
American Quasar Petr.	− 4.66	12/84	− 2.44	12/83
Oak Industries	− 12.11	12/84	− 5.09	12/83
Castle & Cooke	− 1.86	6/84	− 1.08	6/83
Peninsula Resources	NA		NA	
Oxoco Inc.	− 2.64	12/84	− 1.85	12/83
Punta Gorda Isle	NA		NA	
Hunt Int'l Res Corp	NA		NA	
Sharon Steel	− 5.00	12/84	− 3.16	12/83
Tacomo Boatbuilding	− 6.73	12/84	− 4.79	12/83
Buttes Gas & Oil	− 2.90	12/84	− 1.57	12/83
Beker Industries	NA		NA	
Global Marine	− 1.37	12/84	0.86	12/83
Brock Hotel	− 4.52	12/84	0.55	12/83
Macrodyne Industries	− 9.97	6/84	− 7.66	6/83
Pettibone Corp.	− 7.82	3/85	− 2.73	3/84
Elsinore Corp.	− 2.09	12/84	− 0.34	12/83
Elsinore Finance	NA		NA	
Mean	− 5.14		− 2.44	

human resources should be able to avoid defaults, provided it is willing to cut its losses when necessary. For investors who have the discipline to pass up fat yields when the credit protection is too thin, the low-rated sector is still attractive, despite legitimate questions about some of the deals being served up by underwriters.

Default Risk Assessment: Database Sample

As noted earlier, Zeta scores correctly identified Chapter X and XI (now Chapter 11) bankruptcies 95% of the time based on data from one statement prior, over the postmodel development period of 1977 to 1982. The accuracy rate is probably lower if we include the most recent data because firms like Johns Manville, Revere Copper & Brass and Storage Technology were not identified correctly. Of more relevant concern for this study was its ability to "red-flag" deteriorating and defaulting companies with publicly traded, straight debt securities.

The Morgan Stanley High Yield Data Base that we constructed contained 20 issuer defaults involving 30 different straight debt issues. These firms are listed in Table 6-5 with their Zeta scores one and two statements prior to default. The results indicate that all but two of the defaults could have been avoided with a strategy of not including (or selling) a firm's debt when its Zeta score was below zero. The number drops to just one firm (Storage Technology) using a strategy of holding only issues with Zeta scores greater than 1.0. And, if an investment grade triple-B equivalent Zeta score (approximately 2.5) is adhered to, every default would have been avoided.

Zeta score cutoffs of 1.0 and 2.5 are referred to here be cause of their use in Chapters 8 and 9 where we develop investment strategies based on Zeta scores. The number of securities in our data base that were associated with Zetas greater than 1.0 ranged from 56 in 1978 to 123 in 1983. That number continued to increase in 1984 and 1985.

In summary, a fundamental credit approach like Zeta can probably eliminate much of the default risk in a dynamic, actively managed portfolio. It can certainly be argued that other credit evaluation tools can also successfully reduce default risk. The earlier the credit system detects impending defaults, the smaller will be both the realized credit deterioration and principal loss for the portfolio.

Table 6-5.   High Yield Defaults and Prior Zeta Scores (Data Base Firms Only)

Company	Default Date	Zeta One Statement Prior to Default	Zeta Two Statements Prior to Default
AM International	4/82	− 4.60	−0.18
Altec Corp.	9/83	− 9.28	−7.88
Amarex Corp.	12/82	− 1.61	−1.25
Anglo Company	11/83	− 0.15	1.20
Braniff (4 Issues)	5/82	− 5.37	−3.40
Charter Co. (2 Issues)	4/84	0.77	1.40
Emons Industries	4/84	− 4.30	−4.99
Food Fair (2 Issues)	10/78	− 0.61	−0.68
Gamble Skogmo	4/82	− 3.20	−1.58
Grolier (2 Issues)	7/77	− 8.95	−1.73
Hardwicke Corp.	7/83	−10.10	−4.61
Lionel Corp.	2/82	− 1.61	−1.91
MGF Oil	5/83	− 4.19	−2.42
Mego Int'l	3/82	− 7.46	−0.36
Morton Shoes	1/82	− 5.05	−2.72
Storage Technology	11/84	1.63	3.13
Telcom Corp.	12/82	− 4.72	−2.75
Texas Int'l Air	9/83	− 4.11	−4.26
United M&M	7/77	− 0.38	0.24
Wickes Co. (5 Issues)	4/82	− 3.85	−1.17
Average Zeta score		− 3.85	−1.79

7

Mergers and Acquisitions—Recent Experience and Leverage Issues

Heightened activity in the mergers and acquisitions (M&A) area over the last several years has led to an unprecedented level of public awareness and increased regulatory agency involvement. The growing number of multibillion dollar deals has catapulted corporate leverage ratios far above traditional levels. This has caused active debate regarding the tradeoff between the economic benefits of many acquisitions versus the additional company and systemic risk accompanying an increasingly leveraged economy. High yield debt has become the focal point of these rising concerns though it has arguably played a relatively minor role in total dollar terms with respect to completed mergers.

In this chapter we briefly look at (1) the recent growth and changes in M&A activity, (2) the impact on the debt holding investors, (3) the role high yield debt has played, and (4) the several recent changes that may affect future high yield debt issuance and M&A activity in general.

THE RECENT ACTIVITY

The nature of merger and acquisition activity has shifted over the last 20 years from a large number of smaller-sized deals in the late 1960s and early 1970s (peaking at 6,107 net announcements—announced deals less terminated deals—and an average size of $10.3 million in 1969) to a smaller number of much larger deals in the last few years (3,001 net announcements with an average size of $136.2 million in 1985). Table 7-1, compiled by W. T. Grimm (1984), documents the impact of the larger "announced" deals on a total dollar and average deal size basis. In only three years, 1983 to 1985, the total dollars involved in net announced deals more than doubled, moving from $73 billion to almost $180 billion. This in turn caused the average deal size to jump from $67.9 million in 1983 to over $136 million in 1985. The more accurate measure of deal size, median price, jumped 160% from $8.1 million in 1978 to $21.1 million in 1985. The number of net announced deals over $1 billion rose from only one for the entire 1968 to 1974 period, to 18 in 1984, and 36 in 1985. The year 1984 witnessed the two largest deals ever to be announced—Chevron's acquisition of Gulf Corp. ($13.2 billion) and the currently disputed acquisition of Getty Oil by Texaco for $10.1 billion. In order to get a better feel for deals that would have been large enough to justify public debt financing and that were actually consummated, we now turn to completed transactions.

Table 7-2 highlights *completed* transactions of over $35 million and over $500 million from January 1978 through August 1986. The growth in deal size is apparent in both

Table 7-1. Average and Median Purchase Price for Net Announced Deals: 1968 to 1985 ($MM)

Year	Total Dollar Value Paid	Base[a]	Total[b]	Number of Transactions Valued at $100MM or More	$1,000MM or More	Average Price	Median Price
1968	$ 43,609.0	1,514	4,462	46	—	$ 28.8	na
1969	23,710.9	2,300	6,107	24	—	10.3	na
1970	16,414.9	1,671	5,152	10	1	9.8	na
1971	12,619.3	1,707	4,608	7	—	7.4	na
1972	16,680.5	1,930	4,801	15	—	8.6	$ 2.8
1973	16,664.5	1,574	4,040	28	—	10.6	3.4
1974	12,465.6	995	2,861	15	—	12.5	3.6
1975	11,796.4	848	2,297	14	1	13.9	4.3
1976	20,029.5	998	2,276	39	1	20.1	5.1
1977	21,937.1	1,032	2,224	41	—	21.3	6.6
1978	34,180.4	1,071	2,106	80	1	31.9	8.1
1979	43,535.1	1,047	2,128	83	3	41.6	8.5
1980	44,345.7	890	1,889	94	4	49.8	9.3
1981	82,617.6	1,126	2,395	113	12	73.4	9.0
1982	53,754.5	930	2,346	116	6	57.8	10.5
1983	73,080.5	1,077	2,533	138	11	67.9	16.5
1984	122,223.7	1,084	2,543	200	18	112.8	20.1
1985	179,767.5	1,320	3,001	270	36	136.2	21.1

Source: W.T. Grimm & Co.
a Base: the number of transactions which disclosed a purchase price
b Total: Net merger-acquisition announcements.

Table 7-2. M & A Activity: 1978 Thru August 1986[a]

	Aggregate Value ($000)	Number of Transactions	Average Size ($000)
Completed Transactions $35MM or More			
1978	$ 9,142,809	71	$ 128,772
1979	30,719,807	160	191,999
1980	31,702,908	169	187,591
1981	64,236,619	234	274,515
1982	56,887,455	243	234,105
1983	49,788,351	266	187,174
1984	118,084,098	386	305,917
1985	124,701,547	404	308,667
1986 thru Aug 1986	93,900,897	278	337,773
Total	$579,164,491	2,211	$ 261,947
Completed Transactions $500MM or More			
1978	$ 1,598,085	2	$ 799,043
1979	11,870,709	12	989,226
1980	13,417,728	14	958,409
1981	38,390,351	29	1,323,805
1982	29,261,581	18	1,625,643
1983	23,275,979	21	1,108,380
1984	71,749,071	43	1,668,583
1985	75,361,283	51	1,477,672
1986 thru Aug 1986	58,458,268	40	1,461,457
Total	$323,383,055	230	$1,406,013

[a] Source: Morgan Stanley & Co., Incorporated. Exhibits do not include purchases of minority interests, joint venture, buy-backs, or self-tender offers.

the number of transactions over $500 million and the average deal sizes. The oil mega-mergers of 1985 pushed that year's average deal size to over two and a half times that of 1978, while the number of deals grew almost five fold. There were only two completed deals of $500 million or more in 1978 as opposed to 51 in 1985. If we observe deals sizes that might prompt public financing, for example, $35 million or more, the dollar value of completed deals in 1984 and 1985 ($242.8 billion) represents 50% of the value of all deals done between 1978 and 1985 ($485.3 billion).

Observers in the field attribute the recent rapid growth in M&A deals in general, to several factors. First, as domestic markets mature and global competition increases, major corporations have come to accept acquisitions as a legitimate means for growth. In many cases, it may be the only way to make an impact on sales and earnings that run in the billions of dollars.

The stigma surrounding earnings growth driven by acquisitions, a practice used by the aggressive conglomerates of the 1960s, was somewhat dispelled by accounting regulation changes (APB 16 in 1970) designed to better reflect the economic substance of the business combination. These changes gave investors and the businesses themselves a more accurate picture of the impact transactions had on financial statements of the firms involved.

Industry specific deregulation has also had a major impact on the number and size of deals in the oil and gas, banking and finance (including insurance and REITs), transportation, and broadcasting industries. Since 1981, deregulation has led to considerable intra- and interindustry transactions as companies moved to enter these areas or consolidate and strengthen their current positions in them. Such activities have resulted in these industries being well represented in the statistics. According to W. T. Grimm &

Co., these industries alone represented a cumulative total of over 45% of the M&A transaction dollars between 1981 and 1984 (oil and gas alone represented 26%).

Changes in antitrust regulations also played a major role in the consolidation of industries, across the board. In 1982, the Justice Department repealed restrictions against vertical mergers (supplier–customer types). Horizontal merger restrictions, while somewhat relaxed in 1982, were further loosened in 1984 when the Justice Department began using new testing methods for establishing the anticompetitive impact of a given deal. This newfound freedom to buy or merge with competitors has allowed companies (conglomerates in particular) to concentrate their efforts towards their key businesses while divesting those that are more peripheral. These divesture-driven deals have accounted for a significant portion of the M&A activity in the last 3 years.

As the number and size of deals has grown, so has the infrastructure supporting the analyses, execution, and formal combination of the typical deal. Investment banks, law firms, and other consulting oriented companies have greatly expanded their ability to effectively advise clients on all aspects of a deal, thereby increasing the client's "comfort" in executing larger, more intricate transactions.

Another major factor influencing the pace in the 1983 to 1985 period was the substantially increased cash flows many companies generated as a result of inventory and cost reductions implemented during the 1981 to 1982 economic downturn. As substantial cash positions began to build and major internal opportunities for growth were exhausted, companies turned to acquisitions for growth and investment.

Finally, the 1981 to 1982 recession left the market value of many companies' equity severely undervalued compared to their asset liquidation or cash flow generation value, making the purchase of an ongoing entity (at substantial premiums) more economical than acquiring individual assets independently. This was exemplified by a number of major mergers and acquisitions in the oil industry, including the Mobil-Superior Oil and Texaco-Getty deals, and was a major reason for Mesa Petroleum's run at Phillips Petroleum and Unocal. In their cases, oil reserves were more economically acquired via the stock market than by direct exploration. In 1986, however, with stock values reaching record levels, the pace of merger transactions may be slowed as the market value of publicly traded equity becomes more fully valued with respect to the underlying assets. On the other hand, the sharp decline in interest rates (making acquisitions more affordable), will undoubtedly act to stimulate M&A activity.

LEVERAGED BUYOUTS

Table 7-3 highlights the growth of a particular kind of deal known for its heavy reliance on junk bond financing, the leveraged buyout (LBO). In a LBO, a company or subsidiary is taken private in a transaction funded by debt supported by the earnings of the firm itself. Typically, assets are sold off to reduce the initial debt load to manageable levels. Because the company becomes so highly leveraged as a result, its debt ratings (new and existing) frequently fall into the speculative grade category.

The number of completed LBOs grew from two in 1979 to a record 48 in 1984, and then dropped to 34 in 1985. In dollar terms, however, LBO deals represented only 12.3% and 9.1% of the total dollars involved in completed transactions for 1984 and 1985 respectively. The slowdown in 1985 may

Table 7-3. Leveraged Buyout Transactions: 1978 to 1986

	Aggregate Value ($000)	Number of Transactions	Average Size ($000)
	Completed Transactions of $35MM or More		
1978	—	—	—
1979	$ 471,293	2	$235,647
1980	721,953	3	240,651
1981	3,136,298	17	184,488
1982	3,365,175	20	167,809
1983	3,807,671	29	131,299
1984	14,202,457	48	295,885
1985	11,299,446	34	332,337
1986 through (2/28/86)	19,370,418	33	586,982
Total	$56,365,711	186	$303,041

Source: Morgan Stanley & Co., Incorporated.

be, in part, attributable to the increasing cost of acquiring more fully valued shares in the market place. As equity share prices rise, the economics of doing LBOs diminish.

However, renewed growth in this area appears to be coming from lower interest rates and the large number of major funds recently established to finance LBOs. Their primary attraction? High yields plus, in many cases, equity participation. By August 1986 the dollar value of LBOs had already outpaced all of 1985. Critics charge that the quality of LBO deals brought to market is beginning to suffer as the supply of investable funds outstrips the demand. While there was an apparent decline in overall new issuer credit quality in 1985 (something critics may blame on marginal LBOs), a lack of specific data on issue purposes makes it impossible for us to attribute the decline to any specific type of transaction or the credit quality of the companies involved in them.

The net effect of more fully priced shares, lower interest rates, large LBO (and arbitrage) funds, and the other factors mentioned earlier on total M&A activity over the next few years is impossible to accurately predict. But, judging from the creativity of dealmakers and the continued need for corporate growth, both domestically and internationally, it appears likely that deal sizes and numbers will continue to grow with increasing emphasis on the international side.

IMPACT ON PRETRANSACTION INVESTORS

Given the changes in mergers and acquisitions activities, how have investors generally fared when their firm becomes involved in a sizeable deal?

In the case of acquisitions by tender offer, equity holders of *acquired* firms have done far better than their debt holding counterparts. While shareholders frequently receive premiums of between 20 and 70% or more (with the recent average being in the 35 to 50% range), existing debt holders involved in heavily debt-oriented deals typically have to endure rating downgrades, at least in the short term, due to dramatically increased leverage condition, and so, a deterioration in the market value of their holdings. Downgrades, it should be noted, may occur before, during, or after the change in market value.

Returns to equity holders of the *acquiring* firm, however, are more difficult to measure. Bradley (1983) reported that a number of studies show that cumulative abnormal returns (the difference between the expected or normal return and the actual returns observed) on tender offers in general have been positive. However, if one categorizes tender offers by the size of the acquiring firms and compares them on a dollar-weighted basis, it appears that larger acquiring companies show negative returns to shareholders while smaller ones realize substantial gains (enough so as to make the total return on all deals positive). Studies covering mergers are less clear, with some finding positive abnormal returns of up to 10.45% while others showing negative abnormal returns of between 2 to 5%. In most cases as the acquiror leverages up for the acquisition, bondholders suffer.

Obviously not all debt-oriented deals provoke a rating change, but they usually do cause a comprehensive reexamination of the participant's debt ratings. Generally speaking, the larger the acquisition relative to the size of the acquiror the greater the probability of a rating downgrade.

1985 Rating Changes

In terms of rating changes, 1985 was a particularly bad year for existing debt holders involved in mergers, acquisitions, stock repurchases and leveraged buyouts. Standard & Poor's (1986) lowered ratings on 272 corporate issues (industrial, financial, utility, transportation, and foreign), well above 1984's more normal level of 173. Only 125 issues were upgraded, versus 164 in 1984. The credit quality of "industrial" firms took a sharp turn for the worse in 1985, with rating decreases outnumbering increases by nearly four to one (187 vs. 49). Acquisitions, divestitures, leveraged buyouts and stock repurchases accounted for 28% of all industrial debt rating changes and a full 31% of the downgrades. In effect these restructurings accounted for approximately 58 downgrades and only 8 upgrades!

Moody's (1986), on the other hand, raised ratings on 124 issues and lowered 153 in 1985. Fifty-one of the downgrades were caused by restructurings (acquisitions, divestitures, LBOs or share repurchases), with 48 of them being in the "industrial" sector alone. This is opposed to 35 downgrades for the same reasons in 1984.

Table 7-4 highlights Moody's downgrades in more detail. Thirty-three percent of all downgrades due to restructuring affected 38% of the debt involved in all downgrades. In the industrial sector, the numbers are more lopsided. The 48 issues downgraded because of restructuring represented 40% of the industrial rate reductions, but they involved 53% of the total long term, debt dollars whose ratings were lowered.

These statistics present a rather bleak view of the debt holders' position, because they key in on rating changes alone. Fortunately, a fair percentage of deals (generally where the acquirer is much larger than the target or where debt plays a smaller role) result in a reconfirmation of existing ratings. One recently compiled set of statistics helps to get a better, although limited, view of the bondholders' situation.

Standard & Poor's (1985) analyzed a sample of companies in order to assess the impact of acquisitions and divestitures

Table 7-4. Reason Behind Moody's Downgrades—1985

	Companies			Long-Term Debt ($Billions)		
	Restructuring	Fundamental	Total	Restructuring	Fundamental	Total
Industrial	48	73	121	$37.1	$33.4	$ 70.4
Utilities	2	13	15	2.7	22.7	25.4
Transportation	1	2	3	1.0	0.1	1.1
Bank and finance	0	14	14	0.0	10.5	10.5
Total	51	102	153	$40.8	$66.7	$107.5
Percent of total	33%	67%		38%	62%	

Source: Forsyth, R., "Bad Grades—Takeovers Teach a Costly Lesson to Bond Holders," *Barron's*, February 24, 1986.

on the ratings of the companies involved. The results (Table 7-5) show a somewhat brighter picture of the effects acquisitions have on existing bondholders. It should be noted, however, that the numbers include only those companies whose deals caused them to be placed on S&P's *Credit Watch* list (comprised of companies whose ratings are under review) and so may be a biased sample. The reader should also be cautioned regarding a direct comparison between the sample size here and the total transaction numbers listed in Tables 7-1, 7-2, and 7-3. Many, perhaps a sizable majority, of the transactions are between businesses (or involve subsidiaries) with either no S&P or Moody's rating or that have no publicly traded debt outstanding. Many therefore, would not be included in Tables 7-4 through 7-8. While the numbers are small, the sample in Table 7-5 appears to represent a sizable portion of the overall M&A related downgrades in 1985.

Of the 91 issues of *acquiring/divesting* companies put on *Credit Watch* from July 31, 1982 to July 31, 1985, 45% were downgraded. Those deals where ratings were maintained represented 34% while only 12% were upgraded (and most of these were because of divestitures or spinoffs that improved cash positions). Of the 99 *acquired/divested* companies listed, 46% were downgraded, 21% were unchanged, and 18% were upgraded. In all, 46% of the 190 issuers included were downgraded, and 42% remained unchanged or were upgraded. While the investor stands a much stronger chance of a downgrade over an upgrade, he also holds a fair chance of having the current rating reaffirmed.

If one keys in on deals where the issuer was rated below investment grade by S&P prior to the deal, one finds a marginally better picture, with ratings being maintained or upgraded on 49% of the transactions and downgraded on 33%. Unfortunately the sample size is far too small to draw any

Table 7-5. Rating Impact of Acquisitions and Divestitures (For 12 Months Ending July 31)

	Acquiring/Divesting Companies					Acquired/Divested Companies					Combined Total	
	1983	1984	1985	Total	Percent	1983	1984	1985	Total	Percent	Total	Percent
Upgrade	3	2	6[a]	11	12%	7	8	3	18	18%	29	15%
Downgrade	6	19	18	43	47	10	12	23	45	46	88	46
Maintained	9	15	7	31	34	6	7	8	21	21	52	27
Other[b]	1	2	1	4	4	1	8	3	12	12	16	8
Under review	—	—	2	2	2	—	—	3	3	3	5	3
Total	19	38	34	91		24	35	40	99		190	

Source: Standard & Poor's *Credit Watch*, 1985.
[a] Four of these issuers had same parent company (Occidental Petroleum).
[b] Rating withdrawn, issue called, and so on.

formal conclusions from, but the numbers in Table 7-6 may be of interest to the reader.

If one looks at companies crossing the line between junk and investment grades, issuers falling from investment grade into the high yield debt category outnumbered those that rose from junk to investment grade by almost 4 to 1 (Table 7-7). The crossover of investment grades into junk can cause real dollar losses (as opposed to paper losses) to institutional investors governed by policies that force the immediate sale of securities falling below investment grade. Investors with the option to hold high yield debt stand a better chance of weathering what may be a short-term rating downgrade because of a major, debt oriented deal and subsequently recouping their paper losses as the balance sheet improves and prior ratings are restored (or exceeded).

INVESTOR REACTION TO CORPORATE RESTRUCTURINGS

The myriad of downgradings due to corporate restructurings has caused a shift in wealth away from debt holders at least in the short run. As a result, some debt holding investors are switching to the very highest quality credits (i.e., triple-A corporate, treasury and government agency bonds). Others are looking into electric utility issues in order to avoid takeover or LBO related rating reductions. Several new ideas that allow investors to reduce their exposure to this type of risk have surfaced recently. These "innovations" include coupon rates that are subject to change in the event of a major corporate restructuring or recapitalization, put-options on bonds that are exerciseable upon a change in corporate control *accompanied by rating downgrades*, a pledging of assets against the bonds to deter LBO's designed

Table 7-6. Companies with Non-Investment Grade Rating Prior to Deal (For 12 months ending July 31)

	Acquiring/Divesting Companies					Acquired/Divested Companies					Combined	
	1983	1984	1985	Total	Percent	1983	1984	1985	Total	Percent	Total	Percent
Upgraded	—	—	2	2	11%	—	5	2	7	33%	9	23%
Downgraded	1	4	2	7	39	—	2	4	6	29	13	33
Maintained	—	3	3	6	33	1	1	2	4	19	10	26
Other	1	—	—	1	6	—	2	—	2	9	3	8
Under review	—	—	2	2	11	—	—	2	2	9	4	10
Total	2	7	9	18		1	10	10	21		39	

Source: Standard & Poor's, Credit Watch, 1982–1985.

Table 7-7. Acquisition and Divestiture-Related Movement Between Investment and Non-investment Grades

Direction	1983	1984	1985	Total
From investment grade to non-investment grade	4	5	10	19
From non-investment grade to investment grade	0	3	2	5

Source: Standard & Poor's Credit Watch, 1985. For 12 months ending July 31.

to break up the issuing corporation, and others. The impact of these innovations included in covenants in future deals should help to protect investor's capital, but may act as deterrants to future acquisitions and divestitures.

HIGH YIELD DEBT'S ROLE

The role high yield debt has played in the M&A process is unclear as direct relationships between debt issues and completed deals are difficult to identify. The completed deal could have been announced and/or completed before or after the new issues were brought to market. What is clear, however, is the controversy surrounding hostile takeovers using junk bonds as the funding mechanism. The first step could be to look at the amount of debt involved in M&A deals.

While no study has been done to look at M&A related debt as a portion of all debt (for all rating categories), the Office of the Chief Economist–Securities & Exchange Commission (1986) recently released a study on the role of junk bonds in financing successful cash tender offers from January 1, 1981 to July 1, 1986. They studied 272 deals worth a total value of $79.7 billion. Financing for the deals was broken out into four categories: Internal funds, bank borrowing, debt issues, and equity issues. The results showed that from 1981 to 1984 debt issues (all debt assumed to be high yield debt) represented .3% of the total funds ($65 billion) raised. Bank borrowings were a sizable 78.6% of the total.

In the first six months of 1985 however, 13.6% of the $14.7 billion raised was in the form of debt while 77.6% was bank financing. The details are highlighted in Table 7-8.

They also found high yield debt to be more frequently employed in larger and/or hostile tender offer transactions. They concluded that the data "suggests that these changes (increase in use of junk bonds in tender offers) have been less dramatic than public perception suggests." Furthermore, they stated that "high yield bonds are not yet, nor are they likely to become, a dominant force in tender offer financing."

A major and currently unresolved question regards the proportion of bank borrowings that were replaced by longer term, high yield debt shortly after the initial offerings were completed. If a sizable portion was refinanced, high yield debt may have played a much larger role than initial results suggest.

Another approach to examining the role junk bonds have played is to look at the proportion of the total high yield dollars raised specifically for M&A activities. A rough survey, completed by Fridson and Wahl (1986), indicated that in 1985 approximately $6.2 billion of the $14.7 billion in speculative grade debt issued was related to some extent to acquisitions, LBOs, and so on. The authors included debt when the issuing prospectus indicated the proceeds would be used for acquisitions and the issuer had made an acquisition during the 1984–1985 period. They assumed that proceeds from debt issued 12 months before or after an

Table 7-8. Financing for 272 Successful Tender Offers ($ Billions)

Source	1981	1982	1983	1984	1981 to 1985	1/1/85 to 7/1/85[a]
Internal Funds	$ 5.5[b]	$ 1.3	$ 0.8	$ 4.3	$ 11.9	$ 1.0
Percent	26.3	13.8	13.8	14.9	18.3	6.8
Deals	32	22	20	50	124	19
Bank Borrowing	$ 14.7	$ 7.4	$ 5.0	$ 24.0	$ 51.1	$ 11.4
Percent	70.3	78.7	86.2	83.0	78.6	77.6
Deals	41	38	29	65	173	27
Debt Issues	$ 0.0	$ 0.1	$ 0.0	$ 0.1	$ 0.2	$ 2.0
Percent	0.0	1.1	0.0	0.3	0.3	13.6
Deals	0	1	1	2	4	6
Equity Issues	$ 0.7	$ 0.6	$ 0.0	$ 0.5	$ 1.8	$ 0.3
Percent	2.3	6.4	0.0	1.8	2.8	2.0
Deals	1	1	0	6	8	3
Total	$ 20.9	$ 9.4	$ 5.8	$ 28.9	$ 65.0	$ 14.7
Percent	100.0	100.0	100.0	100.0	100.0	100.0
Deals	59	49	36	89	233	39

Source: "Noninvestment Grade Debt as a Source of Tender Offer Financing," Securities and Exchange Commission, Office of Chief Economist, June 1986.

[a] 19 Tender offers have yet to be classified as successful and so are not included here.

[b] Seagram's offer for Conoco represents $2.57 billion of this number.

acquisition was made would have been used, at least in part, to fund the acquisition either directly or indirectly. Because some of this debt could have been used for other purposes, the $6.2 billion total (42% of new junk debt issued in 1985) probably overstates the actual number but gives us a conservative (high) estimate with which to work from.

The preliminary findings of an unpublished internal study by Drexel Burnham Lambert (where 100% of the proceeds of newly issued high yield debt was attributed to the first purpose stated on the offering prospectus), tend to confirm the level found in the Morgan study. Both Morgan Stanley's and Drexel Burnham Lambert's studies indicate that something less than 45% of the straight, high yield debt issued in 1985 went to fund M&A related deals. Difficulties in identifying and quantifying how proceeds are actually used, and the role instruments like private placements with registration rights play, make it almost impossible to get anything more accurate than this type of broad range estimate. Unfortunately, similar figures are not available in the investment grade debt area to allow for comparison, but considering the number and size of the deals being done in that sector, a similar relationship is likely to exist.

Table 7-9 breaks out the 22 domestic deals of over $1 billion completed in 1985, by rating. Only seven of these deals involved acquiror debt below investment grade, and all seven were under $2.6 billion in size. In nearly all cases where ratings were identifiable, the debt of the companies involved was downgraded. The two notable exceptions were United Energy Resources and AVCO (which moved from junk status into investment grade).

Given the recent concern about high yield debt's potentially harmful contribution to an economy becoming overburdened with debt, perhaps an unaddressed issue

Table 7-9. U.S. Industrial Mergers and Acquisitions Completed in 1985—Over $1 Billion

Acquiror	S&P Ratings Before	After	Transaction Size ($ Billions)	Acquired	S&P Ratings Before	After
Philip Morris	A+	A	5.70	General Foods	AA	A
Allied Corp.	A	A	5.00	Signal Comp.	A+	A
General Motors	AA+	AA+	5.00	Hughes Aircraft	—	—
R. J. Reynolds	AA	A	4.91	Nabisco	AA	A
Baxter Travenol	AA−	BBB+	3.80	American Hospital Supply	AA	BBB+
Capital Cities	AA−	A	3.50	American Broadcasting	AA−	A−
Monsanto	A	A−	2.73	G. D. Searle	AA−	A−
Coastal Corp.	**BB−**	**B−**	**2.50**	**American Natural Resources**	**A−**	**A−**
Kohlberg, Kravis, Roberts	**NR**[a]	**NR**	**2.50**	**Storer Communications**	**BB−**	**CCC**
Inter North	A	BBB	2.27	Houston National Gas	BBB+	BBB
Cox Enterprises	NR[b]	NR	2.10[c]	Cox Communications	NR	NR
Pantry Pride	**—**	**CCC**	**1.83**	**Revlon**	**A+**	**B**
Kholberg, Kravis, Roberts	**NR**[a]	**NR**	**1.70**	**Union Texas Petrol (50%)**	**—**	**BB−**
Rockwell International	AA	AA	1.65	Allen Bradley	—	—
Cooper Industries	A	A−	1.50	McGraw Edison	A−	A−
HHF	**NR**[a]	**NR**	**1.45**	**Levi-Strauss**	**A**	**B+**
Farley Metals	**NR**[a]	**NR**	**1.40**	**Northwest Industries**	**BBB**	**B**
Textron	AA−	BBB+	1.40	AVCO	BB+	BBB+
Chesebrough-Ponds	AA−	BBB	1.30	Stauffer Chemical	A	BBB
Procter & Gamble	AAA	AAA	1.24	Richardson Vicks	A	A
MidCon Corporation	BBB	BBB	1.14	United Energy Res.	BBB	BBB+
Wickes	**CCC**	**CCC**	**1.09**	**Consumer/Ind. Prods. Div. of G&W**	**—**	**—**

Sources: Morgan Stanley & Co., Incorporated and Securities Data Corp.

[a] For LBO's that resulted in noninvestment grade ratings, acquiring companies were classified as noninvestment grade even though they had no formal rating.

[b] Classifieds investment grade on basis of P-2/A-2 commercial paper ratings.

[c] Includes holdings already owned by Cox Enterprises.

might be the actual source of this growing debt burden. Major investment grade corporations across the country have been restructuring and acquiring companies of record sizes in the last two years. The effect of this kind of activity on the debt to capital ratios of some major blue chip companies has been dramatic. Companies with impeccable reputations have taken on debt loads far above their traditional level, and far above the average level for industrial firms with comparable ratings. Considering the relative size of investment grade firms to those involved in high yield debt deals, we believe that more attention should be paid to the investment grade players than has been in the past.

HOSTILE TAKEOVERS AND REGULATORY CHANGES

In the last three years, many of the hostile takeovers have involved smaller companies attempting to acquire firms much larger than themselves, using high yield debt backed by the target firm's assets and earning power to finance the transaction (as do LBOs). The result is a highly leveraged entity encumbered with sizable interest payments relative to projected cash flows, thereby substantially increasing the risk of default should an economic downturn occur. Concern about rising debt levels in the economy, along with the increased number of highly leveraged LBOs and takeovers, led federal regulators to take a closer look at the potentially destabilizing impact these types of transactions might have on the financial system as a whole.

During the latter part of 1985, two particularly hard fought hostile takeover attempts, Pantry Pride's offer for Revlon and Mesa Petroleum's bid for Unocal, brought government's concerns to a head, and prompted the Federal Reserve Board to act. On January 9, 1986, the Fed adopted a proposal under which the margin requirement, now applied to stock purchases, would be invoked in certain types of corporate takeovers. By a three to two vote, the Fed extended "Regulation G" securities credit controls to borrowings by a "shell" corporation (without substantial assets other than the acquired stock) to finance a tender offer or other large stock acquisition.

More simply, corporations often establish a subsidiary company or "shell" corporation without assets or operating income, the purpose of which is to acquire other companies. In most cases the debt issued by this asset-less shell is guaranteed by the operating parent or secured by assets of the acquiror. In the case of a number of recent highly leveraged takeovers (usually by financial "entrepreneurs"), the debt issued by the shells are backed only by the earning power and/or assets of the target firms, with little protection afforded to investors by the acquiring parent companies.

Under the new ruling, a shell can finance up to 50% of the acquisition price with loans secured by the target's assets (now considered stock). The remaining portion of the acquisition price must come from or be guaranteed by a parent company with "substantial" assets or cash flow. There are, however, three exceptions:

1. A deal that results in a friendly merger or acquisition agreement.
2. A transaction funded by debt securities issued in a "bona fide" public offering (as opposed to placements with a limited number of investors).
3. Debt securities that are issued only after sufficient shares are tendered to permit a "short form" takeover

(possible only once the acquiror owns at least 90% of the shares).

It is interesting to note that the Board of Governors specifically identified the GAF-Union Carbide and Pantry Pride-Revlon bids as takeovers that would not have come under the new rules as they did not utilize qualifying shell companies. On the other hand, they did state that the acquisition vehicle used by Mesa Petroleum in making its unsuccessful tender for Unocal would have been considered a shell, thereby invoking Regulation G.

The impact of the Fed's ruling will, to a large extent, be determined by the courts. By the Fed's design, the courts will be left with the task of defining what constitutes a qualifying "shell" company. Some observers feel the Fed's action will curtail the use of junk bonds in hostile takeovers. Others contend that it is probable that other avenues or deal structures loopholes will be found that allow such takeovers to continue (e.g., convertible preferreds that convert to debt shortly after deal is done). Whether these alternatives can be done as affordably as straight debt remains to be seen.

INVESTOR IMPLICATIONS FOR THE FUTURE

In the last few years, debt investors in general have been subject to an increased risk of rapid loss in the market value of their holdings because of unexpected acquisitions, takeovers, LBOs, and so on. On the other hand, these activities have helped to expand the number of issuers and issues available to high yield investors, thereby increasing the potential for investment and portfolio diversification.

The advent of (1) higher stock prices, (2) covenants protecting debt holders' principal investment, and (3) the application of Regulation G to takeovers may mean downward pressure on the number of *highly* leveraged takeovers and economically marginal acquisitions but should not substantially affect the growth in acquisitions overall. These changes in the longer run should help reduce investors' risks both of default (due to marginal deals gone sour) and of large shifts in wealth from debt holders to equity holders when major corporate restructurings occur.

On the other hand, large LBO funds may act to destabilize the market if they continue to finance LBOs at even higher P/E ratios and cash flow multiples, making those types of deals even riskier for investors. Also, the steep decline in interest rates in late 1985 may help drive average deal sizes (and leverage ratios on LBOs) to record highs in future years, thereby continuing the trend in ratings downgrades. A major unknown at this juncture is the impact the new tax legislation will have on M&A activity. As the final details are as yet unavailable, its effect on future deals is unpredictable.

Generally speaking, while the Fed's action may make the high yield market a less controversial investment arena, investors are likely to see continued growth in the number and size of the deals being done. With this growth should come an improvement in the depth and diversification potential of the high yield marketplace for investors (i.e. the new debt issued to fund M&A activity). Those pre-transaction investors that have adequate protection from the immediate rating/market price dislocations and can hold on until the financial situation of the issuer/acquiror improves, should find this marketplace increasingly viable in the future.

8

Portfolio Strategies in the High Yield Debt Market

PERFORMANCE MEASUREMENT QUESTIONS

We observed in previous chapters that high yield bonds have provided substantial return premiums to their holders in recent years. Having examined the anatomy, investor, default, and credit aspects of this area, we now turn to specific investment strategies of high yield bonds. Here, we quantify return premiums for different portfolio strategies and also measure additional risk dimensions. In doing so, we hope to answer several key questions.

1. What have been the expected yields and actual returns as well as the variation in these returns for a diversified, passive investor in the high yield market in recent years?

2. Are there ways to improve on the risk/return relationship in this marketplace using specific, active portfolio selection strategies?

3. Can a credit evaluation model be helpful in providing acceptable promised yield and return levels combined with desirable risk reduction qualities?

4. Do high yield debt portfolio strategies demonstrate statistically significant differential returns compared with strategies involving corporate investment grade or government bonds?

These and other factors in measuring performance of investment strategies will be assessed in this and the following chapter.

SUMMARY OF RESULTS

We found that all of our high yield debt portfolios, chosen in terms of various credit criteria, or based on a passive overall high yield debt composite grouping, performed significantly better than both long-term government bond and corporate investment grade portfolios. Our tests adjust for individual portfolio variances as well as the covariance of returns over time between portfolios. Our initial test compares high yield portfolios with a long-term government bond portfolio. We also construct and test, in Chapter 9, a synthetic government bond portfolio; that is, a portfolio combining several types of government securities, in order to approximate the high yield debt groups with respect to average duration. These tests show the superiority of the high yield portfolios although the statistical significance of the duration matched results were lower than the results of the unmatched portfolios.

Finally, we demonstrate that credit risk models such as the Zeta™ credit scores, discussed in Chapter 6, can dramatically reduce the default risk of high yield portfolios without negatively impacting returns. Investors who wish to enjoy the prospect of high yields and returns but desire a "prudent-screen" of individual firm default risk, might be attracted to this procedure. In general our results show that a strategy of investing in "quality junk" bonds is both viable and worthy of serious consideration.

DATABASE PROPERTIES

To answer our four key questions, an analytic data base of 440 high yield bonds was constructed to allow the tracking of period by period results from 1978 to 1984. We refer to results from this data base as our *High Yield Composite*. It was designed to measure key aspects of any chosen portfolio, including average *coupon*, average bond *rating*, weighted and unweighted *returns*, *yields*, *maturity dates*, and *duration*. In addition, the data base had a history of Zeta *credit scores* for each company going back to 1975 as well as the issues' *bond ratings* over time. For details of this data base and calculation procedures, see Appendix 1.

PORTFOLIO CONSTRUCTION AND COMPARISON TESTS

A number of index and strategy based portfolios were constructed and analyzed for comparison. These include:

Constructed Portfolios

1. An index of low rated (double-B or lower) bonds, called the *High Yield Composite* (*HY Comp*)
2. An index for S&P rated bonds *by rating* (BB,B and CCC)

3. Portfolios based on *Zeta scores:*
   a. Zetas greater than or equal to 1 $(Z \geq 1)$
   b. Zetas greater than or equal to 1 with an *uptick* (positive change in Zeta over the prior year $(Z \geq 1+)$
   c. Zetas greater than or equal to 1 with a *downtick* (negative change) from prior year's score $(Z \geq 1-)$
   d. Zetas greater than or equal to 2.5 $(Z \geq 2.5)$
   e. Zeta quartiles (Z Q-1, Z Q-2, Z Q-3, Z Q-4)

BENCHMARK PORTFOLIOS

In addition to the portfolio strategies containing high yield bond issues, we also generate yearly returns and/or yields on *Shearson Lehman's Long-Term Government Index, Salomon Brothers' A-Rated Bond Index, Standard & Poor's BBB Index,* and *S&P's Composite Index of 500 Stocks* (the S&P 500). These portfolios were used as benchmarks for comparison with the custom-built portfolios. Statistical tests were completed on the differences in returns over the six annual periods and 72 monthly periods, incorporating tests to account for covariance effects between strategies.

PORTFOLIO RETURNS OVER THE STUDY PERIOD

We chose 1978 as the starting year due to Zeta score availability and the start of the growth in the high yield bond market. Since Zeta scores for calendar year closings are first available in March, our study period starts on March 31, 1978 and goes to March 31, 1984.

The six-year period was an exceptionally volatile one. Interest rates on the Long-Term Government Bond Index

(LT Gov'ts) rose from about the 8% yield level in early 1978 to record heights, peaking in the third quarter of 1981 at around 15%. One year later, it had dropped to just under 12%. Interest rate volatility caused large variations in bond returns and promised yields. Hence, yield and return spreads, partly due to interest rate changes and differential coupon rates, were also volatile.

Tables 8-1 and 8-2 summarize portfolio attributes and performance measures for the various strategies indicated previously. As can be seen in these tables, 1979, 1980, and 1982 are especially noteworthy with respect to returns. The jump in interest rates during the 1979 holding period caused substantial price deterioration in the fixed income market, leading to large annual negative returns (− 16% for LT Gov'ts and − 15% for the High Yield Composite). The superior coupon payment on high yield debt softened the principal loss, especially for the CCC category. Returns in 1979 varied from − 19.4% for BB bonds to − 10.6% for CCCs. The following year, 1980, saw a reversal for all categories with CCCs again outperforming all other fixed income categories. In that same year, the High Yield Composite experienced a 19.0% return compared to just over 10% for LT Gov'ts.

The most impressive year for returns was 1982 when prices rebounded as interest rates fell dramatically from their 1981 highs. Price appreciation accounted for most of 1982's returns of 38% on LT Gov'ts, 44% on A-rated debt, 48% on the High Yield Composite, and an incredible 76% on CCC rated debt. The percentage contribution to annual returns on specific high yield strategies coming from coupon and price appreciation can be found in Appendix 2. One might be even more impressed since this remarkable performance in 1982 was achieved despite 1982's relatively high default rate (Chapter 5). However, as the largest of the defaults occurred in the beginning of the 1982 period, most of the price

Table 8-1. Investment Strategies: Return Comparison[a]

Strategy/Index	1978	1979	1980	1981	1982	1983	Averaged Returns	Six Year Averages			
								Total Compounded Returns	Compounded Annual Returns	Zeta Score	Standard Deviation[b]
High Yield Composite:	5.85%	−15.07%	19.01%	3.43%	48.17%	9.68%	11.85	79.8%	10.3%	.42	21.00
Number of bonds:	153	203	243	280	286	339					
Shearson Lehman Long-Term Gov't Index:	1.52	−16.06	10.10	7.09	37.82	−1.17	6.55	36.9	5.4	NA	17.81
Salomon Brothers A-Rated Bond Index:	1.41	−19.08	14.05	3.85	43.94	4.26	8.07	45.9	6.5	NA	20.50
Portfolio by S&P Rating											
BB	3.14	−19.41	15.11	5.41	45.48	7.80	9.58	58.2	7.9	1.74	21.08
Number of bonds:	34	51	61	49	55	70					
B	5.78	−13.63	20.78	.25	45.81	10.28	11.54	77.9	10.1	−.35	20.28
Number of bonds:	60	93	114	137	142	150					
CCC	10.73	−10.62	27.75	5.25	76.15	13.82	20.51	166.8	17.8	−2.04	29.99
Number of bonds:	17	14	16	23	21	35					
Zeta scores ≥ 1 only:	5.60	−16.03	13.34	6.75	43.71	9.03	10.40	68.1	9.0	3.25	19.26
Number of bonds:	56	64	75	87	97	123					
Zeta scores ≥ 1 and an increase over prior year:	6.10	−17.11	13.79	8.55	43.76	7.69	10.46	68.2	9.0	3.40	19.55
Number of bonds:	33	43	44	57	71	70					
Zeta scores ≥ 1 and a decrease from prior year:	4.84	−12.77	12.47	3.29	43.58	10.48	10.32	68.5	9.1	3.00	18.57
Number of bonds:	22	20	31	30	26	53					
Zeta scores ≥ 2.5 only:	6.81	−16.62	12.25	8.16	42.95	8.57	10.35	67.8	9.0	4.56	19.05
Number of bonds:	25	36	41	42	55	49					
Zeta scores by quartile											
First quartile (highest):	6.12	−15.67	12.05	7.39	43.88	8.26	10.34	67.7	9.0	3.59	19.16
Second quartile:	4.38	−19.44	19.12	.84	43.88	10.54	9.89	60.5	8.2	.78	21.04
Third quartile:	4.94	−12.86	22.66	4.31	54.97	7.68	13.62	95.2	11.8	−.79	23.19
Lowest quartile:	8.34	−11.81	24.20	.86	50.63	13.33	14.26	104.4	12.6	−2.59	21.52
Approx. number of bonds/quartile:	37	50	60	70	71	84					
S&P 500:	19.99	6.16	40.07	−13.06	44.70	8.71	17.76	144.0	16.0	NA	21.88

[a] Returns are weighted by dollar amounts outstanding and are for 12-month periods beginning 3/31 of each year.
[b] Standard Deviation of returns over six years (based on annual returns).

deterioration actually took place in 1981, or earlier. Hence, investors in these issues did not suffer substantial price depreciation in 1982. Indeed, such issues as AM International, Lionel, Gamble Skogmo, and Wickes recovered nicely. (We assume a sale at the end of the period in which the default took place.)

The returns in Table 8-1 are weighted by dollar amounts outstanding on each issue and were calculated by reconstituting the portfolios at the beginning of each annual period and then observing the return for that period's portfolio. In essence, the portfolio is liquidated at the end of the period and the proceeds reinvested in a new set of securities with the same characteristics.

The number of securities in the various strategies over the sample period range from 153 in 1978 to 339 in 1983 for the High Yield Composite, 56 to 123 for Zetas $\geq$ 1.0, and to between 17 and 35 issues for the CCC portfolio (Table 8-1). The latter, while the best performing portfolio in terms of returns, is reported mainly for comparison purposes, realizing that the small number of issues probably makes investments in that group of securities an impractical strategy.

RETURNS AND YIELD SPREADS

Exhibits 8-1, 8-2, and 8-3 illustrate returns, promised yields, yield spreads off Long-Term Governments, and return spreads off Long-Term Governments from March 31, 1978 to March 31, 1984 for most of the portfolios analyzed. Yields are calculated as of the start of the period, for example, for 1978 it is as of March 31, 1978 and returns are for the period covering March 31, 1978 to March 31, 1979.

The geometric or *compounded* annual return over the six-year period ranged from 5.4% for the LT Gov'ts to 17.8%

Table 8-2. Investment Strategies: Yield (%) and Duration Comparison[a]

Strategy		1978	1979	1980	1981	1982	1983	Average
High Yield Composite	Yield:	10.71	11.52	16.16	15.90	18.62	13.77	14.45
	Duration:	7.87	7.52	6.25	6.12	5.63	6.45	6.64
Shearson Lehman Long Term Govt Bond Index	Yield:	8.38	9.13	12.48	12.77	13.70	10.85	11.22
	Duration:	9.90	9.55	8.04	7.84	7.44	8.44	8.53
Portfolio by S&P Rating								
BB rated portfolio	Yield:	9.80	10.85	14.99	15.12	17.21	13.07	13.51
	Duration:	8.70	7.77	6.57	6.62	5.87	6.39	6.99
B rated portfolio	Yield:	10.83	11.79	16.73	15.96	18.50	14.20	14.67
	Duration:	7.84	7.67	6.23	6.17	5.57	6.27	6.63
CCC rated portfolio	Yield:	12.86	13.38	17.89	17.91	22.70	15.60	16.72
	Duration:	7.16	6.87	5.83	5.63	4.80	5.82	6.02
Zeta score ≥ 1 only	Yield:	9.70	10.32	14.56	14.96	16.78	13.10	13.24
	Duration:	8.50	8.08	6.72	6.56	6.03	6.73	7.10
Zeta score ≥ 1 plus uptick	Yield:	9.52	10.18	14.66	14.80	16.83	13.04	13.17
	Duration:	8.55	8.34	6.82	6.48	6.07	6.75	7.17

Zeta score ≥ 1 plus downtick	Yield:	9.92	10.78	14.37	15.25	16.65	13.15	13.35
	Duration:	8.61	7.19	6.54	6.73	5.95	6.71	6.95
Zeta score ≥ 2.5	Yield:	9.56	10.01	14.36	14.77	16.56	12.99	13.04
	Duration:	8.71	8.20	6.90	6.44	5.97	6.63	7.14
Zeta Scores by Quartile								
Top quartile	Yield:	9.58	10.79	14.37	15.11	16.68	12.99	13.25
	Duration:	8.47	7.74	6.80	6.40	6.04	6.67	7.02
Second quartile	Yield:	10.17	11.38	16.35	15.35	17.47	13.64	14.06
	Duration:	8.37	7.71	6.13	6.53	5.65	6.50	6.81
Third quartile	Yield:	11.43	12.06	17.23	16.19	19.27	13.48	14.94
	Duration:	7.68	7.20	6.05	6.10	5.44	6.50	6.50
Lowest quartile	Yield:	12.10	12.82	17.17	17.01	19.86	15.33	15.71
	Duration:	7.10	7.07	5.84	5.67	5.36	5.98	6.17

[a] Yields and duration are from 3/31 of each year and are weighted by the amounts outstanding.

For 3/31/1978 to 3/31/1984

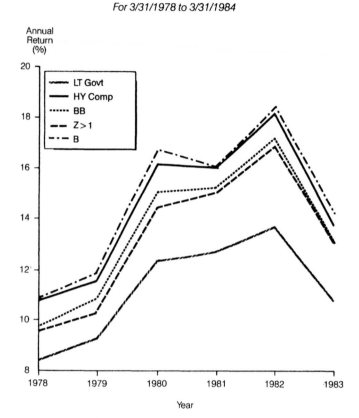

Exhibit 8-1　Annual yield for major strategies.

for CCC. Most of the relevant portfolios returned 8–10% with a few of the higher credit risk portfolios (lower Zeta scores) returning around 12%. *Average* annual returns were somewhat higher for the entire period.

The High Yield Composite averaged 490 basis points (4.9%) in compounded return premiums annually over LT Gov'ts, for the March 31, 1978 to March 31, 1984 period.

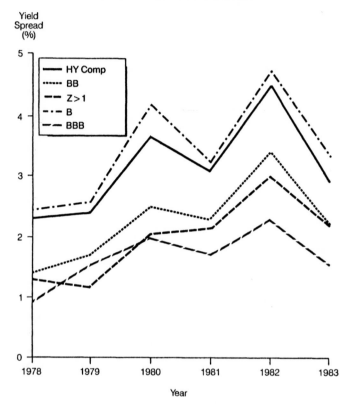

Off LT Govt. Bonds – 3/1978 to 3/1984

Exhibit 8-2   Yield spreads for major strategies.

This premium changed to over 583 BPs when the time pe
riods were moved back 3 months to calendar year periods
(through 1983). The difference indicates the sensitivity of
return calculations to the time frames examined. The average *promised yield spread* over LT Gov'ts was 323 BPs over
the same March 31, 1978 to March 31, 1984 period.

Cumulative (total) and annualized returns are illustrated
in Exhibit 8-4 with each portfolio's average S&P rating. The

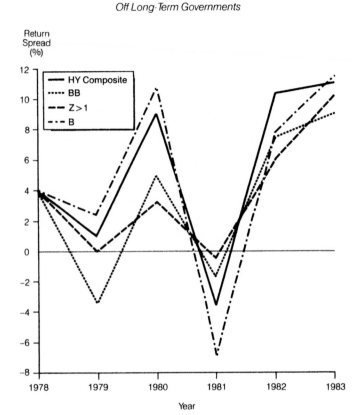

Off Long-Term Governments

Exhibit 8-3   Return spreads for major strategies.

HY Composite's average return was 11.85% (cumulative return of 80%) with an average bond rating of B+.

The return results for portfolios based on Zetas ≥ 1.0 strategies were virtually identical, regardless of whether the score was accompanied by an uptick or a downtick. While we observe that upticks are more frequently associated with rating upgrades than were downticks, it appears that the returns on these higher quality portfolios are primarily im-

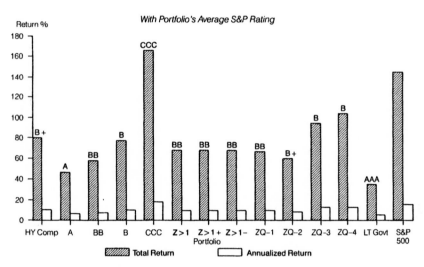

Return %

With Portfolio's Average S&P Rating

Total Return ▨   Annualized Return ▭

Exhibit 8-4   Returns March/1978 to March/1984.

pacted by coupon and interest rate factors and relatively unaffected by credit quality changes. We observe that the quartile separation of Zeta indicates higher returns for the lowest quartiles, no doubt reflecting their lower quality and higher promised yields. It appears that investors in high yield debt reaped higher returns by taking more perceived risks. This is demonstrated by relative spreads on such "high risk" portfolios as the lowest two Zeta quartiles and the CCC category.

The yield spreads are pretty much as one would expect with respect to the various bond rating categories. Table 8-3 indicates that the highest yield spreads (of the rated portfolios) occurred in the CCC portfolio, followed by B and BB. The High Yield Composite can be found somewhere in the middle, on average. Interestingly, the High Yield Composite's *yield spread* for the six-year period (3.23%) was slightly less than the B-rated group (3.44%) while the High Yield

Table 8-3. Yield and Return Spreads by Strategy[a] (Six Year Average Off Long Term Govt. Bonds[b])

Portfolio	Average Return Spread (%)	Compounded Average Return Spread (%)	Yield Spread (%)[c]
Salomon Bros. A Rated Index	1.52 (6 years)	1.1	—
A Rated[d]	−0.01 (5 years)	1.3	—
S&P BBB Rated Index[e]	—	—	1.68
BB	3.03	2.5	2.28
B	4.99	4.7	3.44
CCC	13.96	12.4	5.50
Zeta ⩾ 1	3.85	3.6	2.01
Zeta ⩾ 1 + uptick	3.91	3.6	1.94
Zeta ⩾ 1 + downtick	3.76	3.7	2.12
Zeta top quartile	3.79	3.6	2.02
50–75%	3.34	2.8	2.83
25–50%	7.07	6.4	3.71
0–25%	7.71	7.2	4.49
High Yield Composite	5.30	4.9	3.23
S&P 500	11.21	10.6	—

[a] Holding period March 31, 1978 to March 31, 1984.
[b] Shearson Lehman Long Term Government Bond Index.
[c] Spreads are from average of yields at closing prices on March 31 for each of 6 years.
[d] R. Soldofsky's Holding Period Returns (1984) and data supplied to us by Soldofsky.
[e] No returns available.

204

Composite's *return spread* (5.30%) was above that of the B's (4.99%). The average return was 11.85% on the Composite compared with 11.54% for B's and 9.58% for BB's. All were considerably below the astounding 20.51% for our sample (admittedly small) of CCC rated firms.

The major Zeta strategies, that is, those with the largest number of issues, (Z ≥ 1 and Z Top Quartile) produced *yield* spread levels lower than the BB rated portfolio, but *return* spreads considerably higher. The third and fourth quartile Zeta strategies produced yield spreads between the B and CCC rated portfolios and had returns moderately higher than the B portfolio.

The results thus far indicate that both yield and return spreads of the various high yield debt portfolio strategies are quite attractive. We have not, as yet, tested for the significance of these results nor have we explicitly considered such factors as return variability or exact portfolio matching between junk bond portfolios and the high grade groupings. We now turn to these factors in Chapter 9.

9

Testing of Investment Strategies

We observed in Chapter 8 that a number of strategies in the high yield debt sector provided attractive returns over the period 1978 to 1984. These included passive investment strategies involving analysis of a specially constructed *High Yield Composite* portfolio and also active strategies reflecting selection by credit risk criteria. The latter portfolios represent our attempt to analyze techniques to select securities with high yields and credit risk attributes that are satisfactory to an investor.

The major strategies that we singled out for close scrutiny involved choosing portfolios by bond rating, for example, only BB (Ba) or only B rated bonds, and also strategies based on various Zeta score criteria. The latter strategies involve selecting only those bonds whose company's score was greater than zero or positive 1.0 or 2.5. In addition, we selected portfolios by dividing the entire sample into quartile Zeta scores with the theory that the highest Zeta scores were the best credit risk and conform to higher bond rating equivalents. Implicit in these strategies is the notion that higher

bond ratings and higher Zeta scores mean less defaults and
that the investor can all but eliminate losses coincident with
defaults. On the other hand, higher credit worthy companies probably mean lower *expected* returns.

We hasten to add that while we have chosen Zeta scores
as our investment screen, the professional manager probably has alternative credit screens or, indeed, an in-house
credit department, which can attempt to provide a similar
type of selection criteria. Regardless of the credit screen
selected, however, some additional qualitative and quantitative investigation is recommended as individual issues
are considered. For instance, the liquidity of the issue—
mainly based on the available supply of tradeable debt—
should be ascertained. Or, if there is security involved or a
third party guarantor, then the credit worthiness of the issue
is no doubt heightened. We now turn to an analysis and
discussion of the various strategies and the measurement
and testing of returns on these strategies.

ISSUES IN RISK-RETURN MEASUREMENT

To understand the period-to-period *risk* of a portfolio in
terms of yield and return, we can look at the variance of
these factors over time. Exhibit 9-1 shows the standard deviations in *yield to maturity*, calculated over the six-year
sample period, for a number of high yield debt investment
strategies. As expected, the lower the rating the more volatile the yield and, not surprisingly, the lowest variance in-
volves the Long-Term Government index. The High Yield
(HY) Composite is located approximately where its average
rating (B+) would have predicted it would. One data point
in Exhibit 9-1, SYN Gov't, has yet to be defined and will be
discussed shortly.

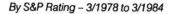

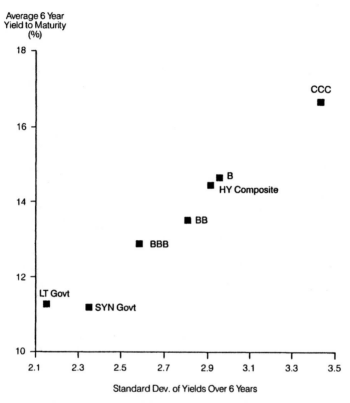

Exhibit 9-1   Standard deviation of yields vs. yields.

The annual *return* deviations, however, show something different. While the averages show increased returns as ratings decrease (except for single-B rated bonds), there is a steep increase in return, with little difference in risk, over the entire A to B rating range (Exhibit 9-2). Indeed, the standard deviation of returns over six years is virtually the same for the different ratings. The only exception is the CCC rated

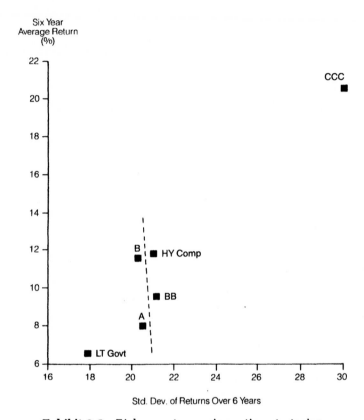

Annual Data – 3/1978 to 3/1984

Exhibit 9-2   Risk vs. return using rating strategies.

category, with a standard deviation of about 50% higher than B, BB and most of the Zeta portfolios.

These return-generated results could be caused by the limited number of data points (6) used in calculating standard deviations. However, the tendency of four of the portfolios (A, BB, B and HY Composite) to have little difference in risk agrees somewhat with the findings of a high yield debt study done by Blume and Keim (1984). They actually found that higher rated debt had greater return volatility than did lower rated debt! This is counterintuitive since most analysts attribute lower risk and volatility measures to investment grade securities than for speculative corporate debt.

In order to investigate this anomaly, we utilized a *monthly* return index so as to increase the number of data points and to allow for direct comparison with the Drexel Burnham Lambert Composite and the Blume & Keim monthly indices.

Upon rerunning the major portfolio strategies using monthly data, the anomaly corrected itself for the portfolios from the Morgan Stanley high yield data base, that is, the ones selected by bond ratings and Zeta. But *Salomon Brother's A-Rated Index* and *Shearson's Long-Term Government Bond Index* showed increased volatility and shifted to the right of even our B-rated portfolio (see Exhibit 9-3). The number of data points does not appear to be the complete answer to the anomaly. However, the Long-Term Government Index has a longer average years to maturity and duration than the other indices, and this might explain the greater volatility in monthly returns. Indeed, when we plot *Shearson Lehman's Short-Term Government/Corporate Index* for *monthly returns*, the standard deviation of returns is lower than the others. We will return to this issue in our section on duration matching.

The previously mentioned empirical observations appear to explain a substantial portion of the anomaly. In addition, there are at least two other sources of bias which could help explain the observed relationships. First, our data may be smoothing prices abnormally, because of its mix of *matrix prices* (that is, prices not observed but determined based on their relationship with other "benchmark" bonds), and *listed prices* on exchanges like the New York Stock Exchange.

Monthly Data: 3/1978 to 3/1984

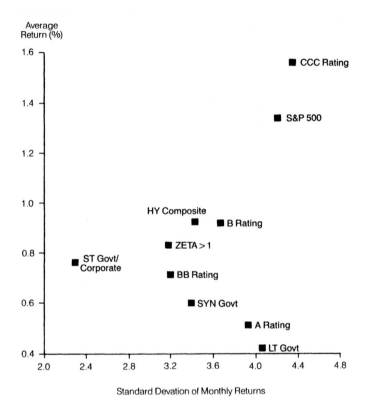

Exhibit 9-3   Average returns vs. standard deviation of return.

This would mean that the traditional risk-return (mean-variance) analysis would be difficult to measure reliably. The Blume & Keim findings could also be susceptible to this problem as they used broker quotes from two different firms (Drexel and Salomon) and took an average when there were differences.

Another explanation for a risk-return anomaly could be

that high yield bonds tend to trade with an equity component that offsets interest rate fluctuations more than anticipated. Investors in high quality bonds tend to key in on
interest rates, placing much less emphasis on credit quality.
Investors in low-rated bonds, however, are usually very
credit-conscious, and look more at the firm's operating fun-
damentals. While a company's stock is generally more volatile than its bonds, stock movements are usually not highly
correlated to minor interest rate fluctuations. An equity
component in low-rated debt may, as a result, help to counter
some of the interest-rate-driven price fluctuations.

Finally, recall that these are *realized* return-risk measures.
The *promised yield versus risk* measures plot consistent
with theory.

ANNUAL RISK-RETURN RESULTS

Using the less controversial (with respect to realized variance of returns) average *annual return* data, Exhibit 9-4
combines all of the strategies tested in the risk-return environment. Exhibit 9-5 does the same with respect to yields.
The bunching of the Zeta $\geq$ 1 strategy and the Zeta top
quartile (Z Q-1) strategy in the lower risk range does seem to
indicate that Zeta can be used to create more stable, and in
some cases, higher return distributions (Exhibit 9-4). Compound returns on these portfolios were an average of 110
basis points higher (annually) than the BB rated portfolio.
The Zeta $\geq$ 1 strategy also outperformed the A-rated and Z
Q-2 portfolios by substantial margins, even though these
latter portfolios registered higher risk levels. The B, CCC,
HY Composite and low quality Zeta strategies (Z Q-3 and Z
Q-4) portfolios had higher returns, but they were also accompanied by higher risk levels.

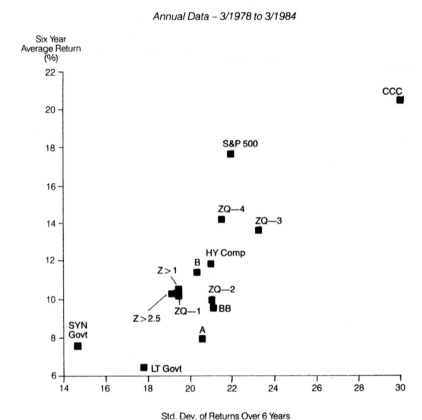

Annual Data – 3/1978 to 3/1984

Exhibit 9-4 Risk vs. return for major strategies.

ZETA STRATEGIES

Zeta score strategies help to screen-out credit risks that have deteriorated and which may be more price-sensitive to adverse company specific or general economic news. Zeta strategies also help the portfolio manager avoid most of the price deterioration immediately prior to bankruptcy and the loss of interest income after the bankruptcy filing date.

By Strategy – 3/1978 to 3/1984

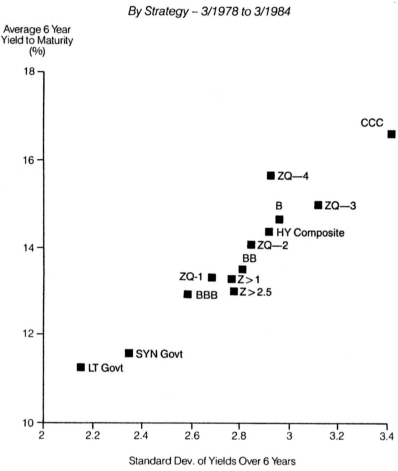

Average 6 Year
Yield to Maturity
(%)

Exhibit 9-5   Standard deviation of yields vs. yields.

In Exhibit 9-4, we note that the Zeta strategy involving Z
≥ 2.5 firms returned the same average annual return (10.35%)
as Z Top Quartile, with slightly less variance and a higher
average Zeta score (4.56 vs. 3.59). This high quality, high
yield strategy, which reduces default risk dramatically,
demonstrated slightly higher average returns and a lower

standard deviation than the double-B rated category and slightly less return and standard deviation of return compared to single-B rated issues. This differential is even more dramatic when compared with the A-rated index. The primary problem with the $Z \geq 2.5$ strategy is the relatively small number of eligible issues (49 at the end of 1983 and 67 in 1984). This is less than half of the eligible issues than we find with the $Z \geq 1.0$ strategy.

In our sample, only one firm, Storage Technology, filed for bankruptcy that had a score greater than 1.0. The other defaulting firms were eliminated from these portfolios once their scores fell below 1.0; however, in many cases their ratings remained at the B level or above until bankruptcy. In effect, Zeta can steer the portfolio manager clear of most potential defaults before dramatically affecting returns. As defaults usually do not come without some prior credit quality deterioration, some price depreciation can manifest even with an accurate default predictor.

The higher quality Zeta strategies produced returns that were nearly indistinguishable from each other (see Table 8-1 in the prior chapter). Yield and return spreads are shown again in Table 9-1. Note that the return spreads for the high quality Zeta portfolios ranged from 3.34% (Zeta 3rd Quartile) to 3.91% (Zeta $\geq 1+$ uptick). The lower quality Zeta quartiles did show higher returns (over 7% spreads).

The Zeta ≥ 1 strategy had the major advantage of providing a larger pool of bonds to draw from. An average of 33% of the sample bonds qualified each year using Zeta ≥ 1 as opposed to 25% for the next largest available pool (Top Quartile), 21% for the Zeta $\geq 1+$ uptick, 19% for Zeta ≥ 2.5, and 12% for the Zeta $\geq 1+$ downtick. As of the end of 1984, there were 138 issues which would qualify for inclusion in a portfolio of $Z \geq 1.0$. Forty of the issues had outstanding amounts of $100 million or more and 78 with $50 million or more.

Table 9-1. Yield and Return Spreads by Strategy[a] (Six Year Average Off Long Term Govt. Bonds[b])

Portfolio	Average Return Spread (%)	Compounded Average Return Spread (%)	Yield Spread (%)[c]
Salomon Bros. A Rated Index	1.52 (6 years)	1.1	—
A Rated[d]	−0.01 (5 years)	1.3	—
S&P BBB Rated Index[e]	—	—	1.68
BB	3.03	2.5	2.28
B	4.99	4.7	3.44
CCC	13.96	12.4	5.50
Zeta ⩾ 1	3.85	3.6	2.01
Zeta ⩾ 1 + uptick	3.91	3.6	1.94
Zeta ⩾ 1 + downtick	3.76	3.7	2.12
Zeta top quartile	3.79	3.6	2.02
50–75%	3.34	2.8	2.83
25–50%	7.07	6.4	3.71
0–25%	7.71	7.2	4.49
High Yield Composite	5.30	4.9	3.23
S&P 500	11.21	10.6	—

[a] Holding period March 31, 1978 to March 31, 1984.
[b] Shearson Lehman Long-Term Government Bond Index.
[c] Spreads are from average of yields at closing prices on March 31 for each of 6 years.
[d] R. Soldofsky's Holding Period Returns (1984) and data supplied to us by Soldofsky.
[e] No returns available.

SIGNIFICANCE TESTING

There are a number of ways of analyzing empirical results on the risk-return performance of our high yield portfolios. From an *absolute return standpoint*, the average annual results for the six-year period of March 31, 1978 to March 31, 1984 are decent but not overwhelming. Most of the relevant portfolios had annual returns in the 10 to 12% range which was, on the one hand, good compared to investment grade fixed-income portfolios, but inferior to the return on common equities for the same period. Indeed, the S&P 500 returned an average of 17.8% annually. Also, since returns on various quality bond portfolios are highly correlated due to interest rate effects, simply looking at the average returns does not reveal the true significance of differential return performance. Finally, the variance of returns over time must be factored in directly in determining whether differences in average returns between portfolios are significant or not.

DIFFERENCE IN MEANS TESTS

With this in mind we now set out to test for differential performance of the various portfolios listed and summarized earlier in Table 8-1; the actual spreads are given in Table 9-1. Specifically, we will assess whether the high yield portfolios demonstrated significantly different returns from our two investment grade series, (i.e., the LT Gov'ts and the A-rated index). We will also assess differential performance between high yield portfolios.

The annual returns on various bond portfolios are *not* independent over time; thus, we must account for the covariance effect in our differential performance tests. Essentially, we must also understand how the different portfolio returns vary. Although there is some legitimate question of the efficiency of mean-variance tests in the high yield segment, we will utilize this framework in our tests (e.g., if hedging strategies which involve short selling the firm's common stock are introduced into a high yield debt investment strategy, even extremely high default risk potential could become acceptable; see Bookstaber and Jacob (1985), for a discussion of controlling the credit risk in such portfolios.

An appropriate test for analyzing return performance across portfolios is the *t*-test on *annual mean difference measures*, of the form

$$t = \frac{\overline{d}}{S_D/\sqrt{n}}$$

$$\overline{d} = \frac{\sum\limits_{i=1}^{n} d_i}{n}$$

$$S_D = \sqrt{\frac{\sum\limits_{i=1}^{n} (d_i - \overline{d})^2}{n - 1}}$$

where d_i = difference in annual return in period i for two portfolios being considered

$\overline{d}$ = average difference between the two portfolios over the sample period

S_D = standard deviation of the annual differences

n = number of periods

For example, if we want to test the null hypothesis that the average annual return on our High Yield Composite compared with the LT Gov't index over the six-year sample period is not significantly different from zero, a *t*-test of the annual differences would provide the answer. The difference in mean returns for these two series are

DIFFERENCES IN MEAN RETURNS

Year	HY Composite	LT Gov't	=	Difference (d_i)
1978	5.85	1.52	=	4.33
1979	− 15.07	− 16.06	=	0.99
1980	19.01	10.10	=	8.91
1981	3.43	7.09	=	− 3.66
1982	48.17	37.82	=	10.35
1983	9.68	− 1.17	=	10.85
Average	11.85	6.55	=	5.30($\bar{d}$)

$$S_D = 5.82$$

$$t = \frac{\bar{d}}{S_D/\sqrt{n}} = \frac{5.30}{5.82/2.45} = 2.23$$

If we believe that the HY Composite can be either above or below the LT Gov't index, a two-tailed test of significance shows that $t = 2.23$ with 5 degrees of freedom (n-1) is significant at 0.07 level, that is, we are 93% confident that the rejection of the null hypothesis did not happen by chance. A one-tailed test, testing just for superior performance of the HY Composite, is significant at the 0.035 level (96.5% confident). Hence, after adjusting for both the covariance effect and risk (variance of return), the results show the HY Composite significantly outperforming the LT Gov't index over the six-year period.

We tested for the differences in the following strategies and found:

Test	t-Statistic	Two-Tailed Significance Level (Percent)
1. HY Composite vs. LT Gov't Index	2.23	0.070
2. Zeta 1st Quartile vs. LT Gov't Index	2.58	0.050
3. Zeta $\geq$ 1.0 vs. LT Gov't Index	2.40	0.061
4. Zeta $\geq$ 2.5 vs. LT Gov't Index	2.50	0.055
5. CCC vs. LT Gov't Index	2.48	0.056
6. A-Rated vs. LT Gov't Index	0.89	0.420
7. HY Composite vs. A-Rated Index	4.37	0.007
8. HY Composite vs. Zeta $\geq$ 1.0	1.10	0.320
9. HY Composite vs. Zeta 1st Quartile	0.98	0.370
10. Zeta $\geq$ 1.0 vs. A-Rated Index	2.50	0.055
11. Zeta $\geq$ 1.0 vs. Zeta 1st Quartile	0.25	0.750
12. Zeta $\geq$ 2.5 vs. A-Rated Index	2.60	0.048
13. CCC vs. HY Composite	2.18	0.080
14. CCC vs. Zeta $\geq$ 1.0	2.05	0.095
15. Zeta 4th Quartile vs. HY Composite	2.18	0.080
16. S&P 500 vs. HY Composite	0.82	0.470

AN ADDITIONAL MEAN-DIFFERENCE TEST

Another test for the statistical significance of the differences in a matched paired sample (i.e., annual mean differences in rates of return) comparison is the "Wilcoxon matched-pairs signed-ranks" test (Wilcoxon, 1964 and Siegel, 1956). This test considers the magnitude of the annual differences in the rates of return as well as the sign of the differences, but concentrates on ranks of the differences, instead of the absolute differences. For example, if we rank the annual differences in returns (ignoring the sign) between the HY Composite and LT Gov't portfolios we find:

Year	Differences (HY-LT Gov'ts)	Rank	Sign of Rank
1978	4.33	3	+
1979	0.99	1	+
1980	8.91	4	+
1981	− 3.66	2	−
1982	10.35	5	+
1983	10.85	6	+
N = 6	T = 2	Significance = 0.035 level	

The relevant statistic is $T = 2$, which is the sum of the ranks of the *smaller* liked-signed ranks, that is, in 1981 the LT index outperformed the HY Composite and the sign of the rank was negative. Because this was the only occurrence of a negative sign, and it was the second rank, the sum of the smaller liked-signed rank is 2. $T = 2$ is significant at the 0.035 level, concluding that the annual mean differences in return between the HY Composite and our LT Gov't benchmark are significant. This result is consistent with the difference in mean returns test, just discussed.

DISCUSSION OF RESULTS

The overwhelming result of these tests is that every high yield strategy performed significantly better than either the LT Gov't or the A-rated index. Our *t*-test confirms these differentials as significant after adjusting for covariance and variance effects. Also, with the exception of the CCC category and Zeta 4th Quartile, none of the high yield strategies performed significantly differently from any of the others. The A-rated versus LT Gov't returns were insignificantly different from each other, but the HY Composite was most significantly higher versus the A-rated portfolios; even more so than the risk-free government index.

Despite the high average annual differential between the S&P 500 Index and the HY Composite Index (5.91% per year), the differential is not statistically significant due to the high standard deviation of the annual differences. Hence, we cannot be confident that a passive investor buying an equity index could expect to continue receiving such sizable premiums over the passive high yield bond investment strategy.

PORTFOLIO RESULTS ADJUSTED FOR DURATION

Duration Comparisons

Up to this point, we have compared portfolio risks and returns for various long-term bond portfolios but we have not matched these portfolios exactly in terms of their maturities or duration. Duration, a price weighted average term to maturity, has interesting patterns in our analysis. The concept of duration, first discovered by Macauley (1938), and revived in recent years, has become an increasingly popular tool of fixed income managers for matching of portfolios and as a means to estimate the volatility or sensitivity of the portfolio's market value to changes in interest rates. It is a particularly useful matching concept for high yield bond comparisons vis-à-vis government bonds and other investment grade portfolios because coupon levels, that is, cash flows, are quite different. Matching by maturities only considers the final cash flow. See Appendix 3 for a technical description of duration.

Dym and Garbade (1984) provide a particularly clear discussion of the duration concept as a measure of the "futurity" of a bond's total payment stream. In essence, if coupon payments are higher over the life of one bond versus another, the futurity of the higher coupon yielding bond is shorter than the lower coupon bond. Hence, most high yield bonds with higher coupons have shorter futurities, or duration, than investment grade debt. They show, contrary to popular belief, that prices of bonds with equal maturities are not equally sensitive to changes in interest rates but if the two-or-more bond portfolios have the same duration, then they will be equally sensitive to interest rate changes. Following on this, the sensitivity of bond prices to changes in interest rates *increase* with its duration, although this doesn't necessarily always hold for increases in maturities. Finally, if an investor buys a bond with a duration equal to the date on which he needs funds, then he or she is not concerned with interest rate changes over the investment period that the security is held. We also describe duration in Chapter 2.

Earlier we saw that the average duration of our portfolios increases as the credit risk is reduced (Table 8-2). For example, the highest six year average duration was for the

Shearson Lehman LT Government Bond Index (8.53 years) followed by the Zeta ⩾ 1.0 plus uptick and Zeta ⩾ 2.5 (7.17 and 7.14 years). Note also that the quartile Zeta duration rankings are highest for the top quartile (7.02 years) and consistently lower as the quartiles also move lower. The same phenomenon is observed as we go from the BB category (6.99 years) to the CCC (6.02 years). It is quite clear that the coupon rate and promised yield are greater as the credit quality of our portfolios diminish. Since higher coupon payments and higher yields to maturity reduce duration, we are not surprised by our results which show that the HY portfolios have shorter durations than the investment grade groupings.

Constructing Synthetic Duration Government Portfolios

We have shown that all of the high yield portfolios have outperformed the LT Gov't and other investment grade portfolios. We have also found that the return volatility of the Long-Term Government portfolio was actually greater than the high yield portfolios when we used monthly return observations. This was consistent with Blume & Keim's (1984) findings, also using monthly data. Could these results be caused by the differences in duration patterns? Will our results still show that the high yield portfolios outperform the risk-free government indexes when we match portfolios by duration?

To answer these questions, we constructed synthetic government portfolios exactly matching them for duration, for each year, to our High Yield Composite Index. We combined the Shearson Lehman Long-Term Government index with their Government Short-Term index so that the weighted average return of the combined synthetic portfolio was based on a duration of 7.88 years in 1978, 7.52 years in 1979, and so on. The six-year-average duration was therefore equal to 6.64 years for our synthetic government portfolio—exactly the same as our High Yield Composite. In each year, the weightings were approximately two-thirds long term and one-third short term, with 1978 and 1979 showing a 70 to 30% split and 1982 showing a 62 to 38% split.

Table 9-2 indicates the realized annual rates of return and standard deviation of return on our High Yield Composite portfolio and the Synthetic Government Bond Index as well as the LT Gov't grouping, with the yearly duration noted. The average annual return for the High Yield Composite was 4.27% greater than the synthetic portfolio's return. Recall that the High Yield Composite's differential with the LT Government index was even greater, at 5.30%.

The new synthetic government portfolio's (SYN Gov't) yield to maturity versus standard deviation of the yields was indicated in Exhibit 9-1. The monthly return data is

Table 9-2. Annual Rates of Return for the Synthetic Government Bond Portfolio (Matched To HY Composite by Duration)

Year	Duration (years)	HY Comp Return (%)	SYN Gov't Return (%)	LT Gov't Return (%)
1978	7.88	5.85%	2.41%	1.52%
1979	7.52	−15.07	−11.55	−16.06
1980	6.24	19.01	11.32	10.01
1981	6.11	3.43	8.83	7.09
1982	5.63	48.17	32.79	37.82
1983	6.45	9.68	1.66	− 1.17
Average	6.64	11.85	7.58	6.55
Standard Deviation		21.00	14.69	17.82

given in Table 9-3 and the averages plotted in Exhibit 9-3. The annual return and standard deviation of return results are indicated in Exhibit 9-4 and Table 9-2. We observe that both the monthly and annual risk-return results are more in line with expectations, especially in the annual results where the Synthetic Government returns are lower and less volatile than the high yield portfolios. The *monthly* standard deviation of return for the Synthetic Government (3.34%) is considerably lower than the Long-Term Index but very similar to our high yield portfolios. It appears that some of the monthly risk-return anomaly can be explained by the *duration effect*.

We next tested the statistical significance of the average annual and average monthly return differences between our High Yield Composite and the Synthetic Government Index. We find that the average *annual* HY Composite return (11.85%) versus the average annual SYN Gov't return (7.58%) is still significant but less so than the LT Gov't index comparison. The t-test statistic is lower at $t = 1.47$, indicating a significance level at the 0.10 level (90% confident); as compared to the 0.035 level for earlier tests on the LT Gov't index versus the HY Composite index.

The average monthly return for the HY Composite was 0.92% (3.42 standard deviation) compared to the SYN Gov't's 0.60% return (3.34 standard deviation). The monthly differences result in $t = 1.30$, which is also significant at the 0.10 level. When we tested the monthly return difference with the Wilcoxon test, we found higher confidence levels with $t = 1.73$, significant at the 0.08 level.

We therefore continue to find that the HY Composite outperforms the risk-free government bond portfolios, but somewhat less so when the various portfolios are matched for duration. We would like to emphasize the importance of duration matching for fixed income portfolio performance

Table 9-3. Monthly Rates of Return for the High Yield Composite and Synthetic Government Portfolios

Month	HY Comp Return	SYN Gov't Return	Month	HY Comp Return	SYN Gov't Return
4/78	0.02%	−0.02%	4/81	−2.47%	−4.13%
5/78	−1.58	−0.43	5/81	2.29	4.86
6/78	1.09	−0.41	6/81	3.20	−1.05
7/78	1.79	1.17	7/81	−3.01	−2.51
8/78	2.98	1.85	8/81	−2.80	−3.04
9/78	0.43	−0.35	9/81	−2.79	−0.67
10/78	−6.58	−1.70	10/81	2.94	6.58
11/78	1.76	1.12	11/81	9.49	9.42
12/78	−0.39	−1.16	12/81	−3.32	−3.94
1/79	5.49	2.01	1/82	0.50	0.37
2/79	−0.37	−0.63	2/82	0.64	1.80
3/79	2.33	1.01	3/82	−0.23	1.86
4/79	0.33	−0.32	4/82	2.93	2.96
5/79	0.02	1.90	5/82	1.57	1.10
6/79	2.41	2.52	6/82	−1.05	−1.81
7/79	0.36	−0.26	7/82	3.70	4.51
8/79	0.51	−0.40	8/82	8.27	6.24
9/79	−2.67	−0.65	9/82	3.47	5.06
10/79	−7.61	−6.99	10/82	4.55	6.75
11/79	4.37	3.02	11/82	3.96	0.23
12/79	−1.20	0.52	12/82	1.55	2.20
1/80	−0.87	−4.68	1/83	4.95	−1.53
2/80	−6.12	−6.82	2/83	3.73	3.74
3/80	−5.57	0.37	3/83	3.94	−0.35
4/80	13.13	12.38	4/83	4.65	3.05
5/80	5.85	4.38	5/83	−0.90	−2.47
6/80	2.43	2.29	6/83	−0.27	0.35
7/80	−1.92	−2.66	7/83	−0.63	−3.52
8/80	−2.17	−3.83	8/83	1.03	0.55
9/80	−0.81	−1.90	9/83	2.11	3.99
10/80	−0.01	−1.81	10/83	0.35	−0.56
11/80	−1.26	0.49	11/83	1.27	1.56
12/80	−1.42	3.13	12/83	0.11	−0.20
1/81	2.23	−0.53	1/84	2.92	1.88
2/81	0.07	−2.77	2/84	−0.16	−1.22
3/81	3.10	2.72	3/84	0.47	−1.52
			Average	0.92%	0.60%
			Standard Deviation	3.42%	3.34%

comparison. Investors should be made aware of the duration characteristics of different alternative portfolios to better understand the risk and return attributes of his or her options.

VIABLE PORTFOLIO STRATEGIES

At least three portfolio strategies surface with attractive performance, liquidity, and risk of default attributes. These are the

1. High Yield Composite
2. $Z \geq 1.0$
3. Z Top Quartile

The High Yield Composite consisted of at least 350 issues as of the end of 1984 and would number well over 500 issues in early 1986. This comprehensive, passive approach would require the least analytical expenses but transaction costs might be the highest of all strategies. The expected default rate should approximate the high yield default experience and would no doubt be greater than the rate for the $Z \geq 1.0$ or Zeta Top Quartile determined portfolios.

The Zeta ≥ 1.0 portfolio has excellent default risk attributes but the number of eligible securities might not be sufficient for a large fund to continuously channel proceeds into. There were 138 issues at the end of 1984 that met the $Z \geq 1.0$ criterion. About 40 issues had $100 million or more outstanding and another 38 had $50 to 100 million. The Zeta ≥ 2.5 strategy had only about 50 issues that were eligible, while the Zeta Top Quartile had under 100 issues eligible.

An alternative to the $Z \geq 1.0$ criterion would be a portfolio made up of the top one-half Zeta issues. This portfolio did not perform as well (not reported) as $Z \geqslant 1.0$ or even the top quartile index, but would have over 180 eligible issues.

SOME RECENT PRELIMINARY RESULTS USING ZETA

The portfolio performance evaluation period discussed thus far, in Chapters 8 and 9, ended in March 1984 which was the terminal date in our database. We also simulated several of the Zeta strategies for 6 month and 12 month periods in 1985. Our sample size was limited to single issues for each company and, of course, necessitated the availability of Zeta scores.

Out of a relatively small sample of 71 bonds, with the necessary data for the 12 month period of January 1, 1985 to December 31, 1985, 13 had Zetas $\geqslant 1.0$. The average rate of return on this sample was 24.5% compared to 20.8% for the entire 71 high yield bond sample. Recall from Chapters 2 and 4 that the average mutual fund performance in 1985 was 21.7%. The duration of the Zeta $\geqslant 1.0$ portfolio was slightly greater than the all high yield bond sample. As this is just one observation period and the sample size is relatively small, one cannot make any generalizations about expected continued relative performance. Still, it is encouraging to observe these recent results.

HIGH YIELD–HIGH DEFAULT RISK PORTFOLIOS

As indicated earlier, two of the high yield portfolios performed significantly better than the others. These are the

CCC rated group and Zeta 4th Quartile. Both had the greatest default rate but a combination of offsetting higher returns and the one-year holding periods mitigated the impact of defaults. It is important to point out these differences to investors and to offer a broad range of options. Finally, one should match these options with investor utility functions, especially when it comes to risk attributes on speculative bond portfolios.

We also have not explored analytic techniques for achieving efficient portfolios in the traditional mean-variance framework. Preliminary work by Bookstaber and Jacob (1985b) indicates that (1) randomly selected portfolios can achieve minimum variance of returns with as little as fourteen (14) debt securities and (2) adding a large number of issues may actually increase return variability. In addition, a potentially important dimension relating to "systematic crisis risk" for a large number of securities has not been explored. For example, a question can be asked as to what impact a $5 per barrel change in oil prices will have on the default risk of a diversified portfolio. Other examples are the impact of domestic changes in inflation and real interest rates on portfolio returns. Finally, such other factors as principal repayment schedules of the individual issues could be relevant.

HIGH YIELD–HIGH QUALITY PORTFOLIOS— A CONCLUDING NOTE

We have demonstrated that high yield portfolios with minimal default risk qualities (high quality approach) can be achieved with some type of credit evaluation methodology. Returns significantly above investment grade debt securities were observed for portfolios based on the computerized credit screen Zeta technique. If such an approach were adopted, we recommend that traditional, subjective credit evaluation techniques, inherent in a sophisticated credit research environment, complement the computerized approach for at least three reasons:

1. To provide more timely modifications to the portfolio as conditions change between the reporting period of the model

2. To monitor results, especially when a large financial statement data base, such as *Compustat*, reports abnormal results, for example, large annual changes in a company's credit profile

3. To add securities to the "acceptable list" for a fund when the computerized model would not have selected the security. For example, to include securities where data is insufficient to provide a Zeta score, or the firm is not covered by the data base, or the credit deterioration risk is deemed acceptable based on qualitative assessments, and so on.

As in most risk-return frameworks, the greater the risk reduction qualities of an approach, the greater will be the sacrifice in promised yields and also (as based on our findings), the lower the realized expost returns. It remains up to the investor or portfolio manager to reach an appropriate balance between risk and return given the needs of the constituency being served.

Appendix 1

Data Base Characteristics and Calculations

The following is a description of our data base and a discussion of comparisons with other, similar composites.

ANALYTIC METHODS–RETURN CALCULATIONS

For the purposes of portfolio comparisons, the individual period lengths analyzed are restricted to 12 months. The data base can, however, accommodate varying period lengths based on 6-month intervals of time. The time period for calculating returns covered by the study is March 31, 1978 through March 31, 1984. In addition, **monthly wealth indices** are analyzed.

Our **High Yield Composite Index** is based on a weighted average return calculation of individual bonds (coupon and reinvestment income + change in price)/beginning investment, weighted by dollar amounts outstanding and then summed over the entire portfolio.

Bonds pay coupons on different dates over the calendar

year. Within portfolios, coupon income payments arrive throughout the year. This study assumed all coupons, on average, would be paid 6 months into each holding period. The coupon income was immediately reinvested in the same bond until the end of the calculation period. At period's end, the portfolio was sold and reconstructed for the next period. Symbolically, the rate of return on an individual bond can be represented as:

$$R_{i,t} = \frac{(1 + \frac{1/2\ C}{(P_6)})(1 + \frac{1/2\ C}{(P_{12})})\ P_{12}}{P_0} - 1$$

where $R_{i,t}$ = Return on bond i in month t
$\quad\quad C$ = Coupon Amount
$\quad\quad P_0$ = Price at start of month
$\quad\quad P_6$ = Price at end of 6 months
$\quad\quad P_{12}$ = Price at end of 12 months

Defaulting bonds were included in the portfolio up until the end of period in which they defaulted. When a default occurred, one half of coupon income due for the 6-month period (in which the default occurred) was assumed to be received on all issues outstanding for the defaulting company. No additional coupon income was received. At the end of the period, the bond was sold. Bonds in default at the beginning of a new period were not included in the new portfolio. This is an arbitrary assumption and in many cases defaulted bonds can be bought or sold on a postdefault basis.

MONTHLY RETURN INDEX

A monthly return index was also calculated for each of the major portfolio strategies tested. These returns were derived using the following simplified approach:

$$R_{i,t} = \frac{1/12\ C + P_1 - P_0}{P_0}$$

where $R_{i,t}$ = Return on bond i in month t
C = Coupon Amount
P_1 = Price at end of month
P_0 = Price at beginning of month

This methodology, while not perfectly accurate for calculating total compounded returns over longer periods of time (due to our use of a proxy for accrued interest), does provide a good indication of the month-to-month variations in returns. To verify the reliability of our results, we compared our monthly High Yield (HY) Composite to those of Blume & Keim (1984) and also the monthly returns published by Drexel Burnham Lambert (DBL). As noted below, we found the three series to be very highly correlated for the period January 1982 to March 1984.

	Correlation Coefficient (R)
Morgan Stanley HY Composite vs. Blume & Keim Index	.95
Morgan Stanley HY Composite vs. DBL Index	.93
Blume & Keim Index vs. DBL Index	.95

We also calculated the correlation between these three

indexes and Shearson Lehman's Long-Term Government Bond Index, and found significant but lower correlations.

SAMPLE DESCRIPTION

The sample consisted of 440 fixed rate bonds representing 244 issuers from the high yield universe as it existed between 1978 and 1984. Bonds qualified for the sample only if their issuer had a Zeta score for 5 or more years. The model is not appropriate for utilities and financial firms so these were removed. Also, in a handful of cases when companies merged and the debt was assumed, the Zeta score of the parent firm was extended to the merged (issuing) firm from the point of merger onward. Our sample represented, on average, 62% of the total debt outstanding in the low rated universe with utilities comprising the bulk of the bonds not included.

The study sample consisted of 16 industry categories, the largest of which were: manufacturing/heavy industry (61 issuers), conglomerates/(nonbank) holding companies (36 issuers), oil and gas (36 issuers), and high-tech/communications (33 issuers).

DATA BASE INFORMATION SOURCES

Totally reliable pricing in the high yield bond area is probably impossible to find. In the past, because of a lack of interest in the area, very few of the bonds were directly priced, except when a transaction occurred. Because the majority of the study's bonds are traded on the New York and American Exchanges, it was felt that exchange-based prices would give a less biased view of actual market fluctuations than either pure matrix prices or "broker's quotes."

Matrix models use specific "bellwether" bonds and also the yield curve to drive the prices of all other bonds (based on their relative coupons, ratings, level of subordination, maturity dates, etc.). Using pure matrix prices would have meant that prices are determined more by mathematical models than by the characteristics of the high yield market itself. Broker quotes have their own individual bias. "Quotes" can also incorporate a large degree of matrix pricing and may not be continuous due to lack of trading activity.

Our bond price data was derived from the data tapes of the Interactive Data Corp. which essentially provides exchange-listed prices with a small amount of matrix prices. Month-end closing prices or the price closest to the month-end were used. In the majority of cases we had only "ask" prices which could have presented some bias but it turns out the correlation of these prices was very high with Blume & Keim's (1984) broker quote prices.

We also considered using data based on a combination of broker quotes and matrix prices and ran some tests to determine differences in the two data bases. Monthly prices on 12 bonds were compared over the period 1975 to 1984 with 46% of the prices matching exactly and 37% having prices within $20 of each other. Given the close correlation of the two types of pricing available, the decision to use the exchange price data base was a pragmatic one since more complete data histories were available.

Outstanding dollar amounts of each issue came from the May issues of Standard & Poor's Bond Guide and the bond ratings were taken from the July issues of S&P and Moody's (consistent with our earlier default rates (Chapter 5). The May issue was used because of specific investment timing assumptions since the year-end Zeta is not available until April, at the earliest, and investment decisions would have to wait at least until this date.

Appendix 2

Contribution
of Total Return
from Coupon (*C*)
and Price Changes (*P*)

Contribution of Total Return from Coupon (C) and Price Changes (P)[a] (March 1978 to March 1984)

Portfolio	1978		1979		1980	
	C	P	C	P	C	P
High Yield Composite	181.39%	−81.39%	−66.27%	166.27%	80.90%	19.10%
BB Rated	299.03	−199.03	−50.41	150.41	92.30	7.70
B Rated	188.57	−88.57	−76.56	176.56	79.59	20.41
CCC Rated	102.70	−2.70	−95.87	195.87	53.43	46.57
Zeta ⩾ 1	172.64	−72.64	54.90	−154.90	98.87	1.13

Portfolio	1981		1982		1983	
	C	P	C	P	C	P
High Yield Composite	454.69%	−354.69%	39.17%	60.83%	134.94%	−34.94%
BB Rated	283.73	−183.73	38.60	61.40	164.69	−64.69
B Rated	3,041.73	−2,941.73	41.70	58.30	127.75	−27.75
CCC Rated	295.10	−195.10	31.88	68.20	105.52	−5.52
Zeta ⩾ 1	226.79	−126.79	39.44	60.56	140.32	−40.32

[a] The numbers indicate the percentage of total return attributable to coupon income and price changes, and were calculated as follows:

$$\frac{\text{Total Coupon Return (\%)}}{\text{Total Return (\%)}} = C \qquad \frac{\text{Total Return (\%) from Price Change}}{\text{Total Return (\%)}} = P$$

$$\text{Example:} \quad \begin{array}{ll} \text{Total Return} & = 9\% \\ \text{Coupon Return} & = 12\% \\ \text{Price Return} & = -3\% \end{array} \qquad \frac{12\%}{9\%} = 133.33\% \ (C) \qquad \frac{-3\%}{9\%} = -33.33\% \ (P)$$

Appendix 3

Duration and Zero Coupon Bond Equivalency

Frederick Macaulay (1938) developed the duration concept in his search for a correct measure of the life of a bond. Term to maturity is an unambiguous measure of the life of a zero coupon (pure discount) bond. But, because term to maturity ignores the amount and timing of all cash flows save the final payment, it incompletely measures the life of a coupon bond. Macaulay decided to standardize coupon bond life using a zero coupon bond equivalent term to maturity. This reasoning is compelling both because the term to maturity of a zero coupon bond unambiguously measures this bond's life and because any coupon bond might best be viewed as nothing more than a bundle of zero coupon bonds.

The trick Macaulay faced was how to average the maturities of zero coupon bundles. For example, a $100 coupon bond currently at par that pays $10 in interest annually for

This Appendix is reproduced with permission from Toevs, Aldon, "Measuring and Managing Interest Rate Risk: A Guide to Asset/Liability Models Used in Banks and Thrifts," Morgan Stanley & Co., Incorporated, October 1984.

five years may be regarded as a portfolio of five zero coupon bonds: $10 face value zeros maturing in 1, 2, 3, and 4 years and a $110 face value zero maturing in five years. One summary measure of these five maturity dates is three years, which is the simple average of the dates. This approach, however, fails to recognize the different dollar values of the constituent zero coupon bonds.

Weighted Averages of Cash Flow Dates

More reasonable summary measures of a coupon bond's life compute the average term to maturity using dollar weights. Two possible dollar weighting schemes come immediately to mind. First, the dollar weights could be computed by dividing each cash inflow by total cash to be received. For our five-year coupon bond, this dollar weighted average term (WAT) to maturity would be

$$WAT = \frac{10}{150} \times 1 \text{ yr} + \frac{10}{150} \times 2 \text{ yr} + \frac{10}{150} \times 3 \text{ yr} + \frac{10}{150} \times$$

$$4 \text{ yr} + \frac{110}{150} \times 5 \text{ yr} = 4.33 \text{ years}$$

Second, the dollar weights could be computed using present values of future cash flows. Because the present value of any single cash flow is the price of a zero coupon bond with a face value equal to this cash flow, these dollar weights are zero coupon bond price weights. For our example bond, this price weighted average would be

$$D = \left[\frac{10/1.10}{P} \right] 1 \text{ yr} + \left[\frac{10/1.10^2}{P} \right] 2 \text{ yr} + \left[\frac{10/1.10^3}{P} \right] 3 \text{ yr} +$$

$$\left[\frac{10/1.10^4}{P} \right] 4 \text{ yr} + \left[\frac{110/1.10^5}{P} \right] 5 \text{ yr} = 4.16 \text{ years}$$

It was this formulation Macaulay derived and called duration. The weights in this average are given in brackets. The numerator of each weight is the price of the zero coupon bond (i.e., its present or discounted value). The denominator is the *total* present value of all five zeros, which is the price of the coupon bond (P). Given our coupon bond was previously assumed to be trading at par, price is $100.

The price weighted average term to maturity or duration is a superior measure to the WAT. Duration is an average that uses dollar weights computed relative to today's date (present values) and time to receipt of cash computed from today's date. On the other hand, the WAT is internally inconsistent. It computes the time to cash receipt from today's date but the dollar weights do not depend upon today's date.

The duration of any series of cash flows ending at date t_N years can be represented in general terms as

$$D = w_1 \times t_1 + w_2 \times t_2 + w_3 \times t_3 + \ldots + w_N \times t_N \quad (1)$$

Where w_i is the price of the zero coupon bond maturing at date t_i relative to the total price of the bundle of N zero coupon bonds hypothetically comprising the coupon bond.

As a price weighted average term to maturity, duration is measured in years. The duration of a zero coupon bond is its maturity date. (In Equation (1), all weights for a zero coupon bond maturing in t_N years are zero except W_N, which equals 1.0.) Any series of cash flows with a terminal flow at t_N will have a duration less than t_N. The smaller are the dollar flows occurring before t_N, the smaller are these cash flow weights and the closer the duration comes to t_N years. The relationships among the coupon rate (size of intermediate cash flows), yield to maturity, maturity date and duration are depicted in Exhibit A3-1.

The duration of a portfolio of coupon bonds can be com-

Table A3-1. Duration of a $100 Face Value Bond Paying a 7% Coupon (Bond Priced to Give a 10% Yield to Maturity)

Cash Inflow Date	Cash Inflow Amount	Cash Inflows Discounted at 10%	Price Weights	Price Weighted Maturities
0.5 years	$ 3.50	$ 3.34[a]	.036[c]	.018 years[d]
1.0	3.50	3.18	.034	.034
1.5	3.50	3.03	.033	.050
2.0	3.50	2.89	.031	.062
2.5	3.50	2.76	.030	.075
3.0	103.50	77.76	.836	2.508
		$92.96[b]	1.000	2.747 years[e]
		(Current Price)		(Duration)

[a] $3.50/(1.10).5
[b] Current price sums all cash inflows discounted by the yield to maturity (10%).
[c] $3.34/$92.96
[d] .036 × 0.5 years
[e] Duration is the sum of all price weighted maturities.

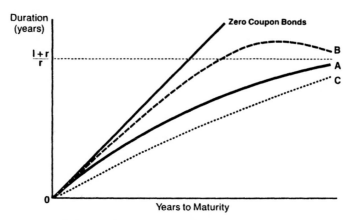

- Duration is related to years to maturity linearly for zero coupon bonds
- OA gives the duration versus maturity relationship for <u>current coupon</u> bonds (bonds priced at par)
- OB gives the duration versus maturity relationship for <u>discounted coupon</u> bonds
- OC gives the duration versus maturity relationship for <u>premium coupon</u> bonds

All coupon bonds have an upper limit to their duration as the maturity date became very distant. This upper limit is the number resulting from computing $(1 + r)/r$

Exhibit A3-1   Duration versus length of time to maturity.

puted using Equation (1) considering all cash flows generated by the portfolio. Oftentimes an easier approach first computes the duration of each coupon bond in the portfolio separately and then makes use of the additivity characteristic of duration to find the duration of the entire portfolio. Additivity means that the duration of a portfolio is the price weighted average of the coupon bond durations. For example, a portfolio of $1000 invested in three-year duration coupon bonds and $2000 in four-year duration coupon bonds has a portfolio duration of D_p = ($1000/$3000) × 3 yrs + ($2000/$3000) × 4 yrs = 3.67 years.

References and Bibliography

Altman, Edward I., "Bankrupt Firms' Equity Securities as an Investment Alternative," *Financial Analysts Journal*, July–August 1969.

Altman, Edward I., *Corporate Financial Distress*, New York: Wiley, 1983.

Altman, Edward I., "Testimony on the Impact of High Yield Bonds on Credit Markets" before the House Subcommittee on Banking, Finance and Urban Affairs, Washington, D.C., September 19, 1985.

Altman, Edward I. (ed.), *The Handbook of Corporate Finance*, New York: Wiley, 1986.

Altman, Edward I. (ed.), *The Handbook of Financial Markets and Institutions*, New York: Wiley, 1986.

Altman, Edward I., R. Haldeman, and P. Narayanan, "Zeta™ Analysis, A New Model to Identify Bankruptcy Risk of Corporations," *Journal of Banking and Finance*, June 1977.

Altman, Edward I., and S.A. Nammacher, "The Default Rate Experience on High Yield Debt," Morgan Stanley & Co., Incorporated, New York, March 1985 and *Financial Analysts Journal*, July–August 1985.

Altman, Edward I., and S.A. Nammacher, "The Anatomy of the High Yield Debt Market," Morgan Stanley & Co., Incorporated, New York, September 1985 and "Update 1985," June 1986.

Atkinson, T.R., "Trends in Corporate Bond Quality," *National Bureau of Economic Research 1967*.

Blume, M.E., and D.B. Keim, "Risk and Return Characteristics of Lower-

Grade Bonds," Working paper, *Rodney White Center for Financial Research*, Wharton School, Philadelphia, PA, 1984.

Bookstaber, R., and R. Clark, "Problems in Evaluating the Performance of Portfolios with Options," *Financial Analysts Journal*, January–February 1985.

Bookstaber, R., and David Jacob, "Risk Management for High Yield Portfolios," Morgan Stanley & Co., Incorporated, New York, January 1986.

Bookstaber, R., and David Jacob, "The Composite Hedge. Controlling the Credit Risk of High Yield Bonds," Morgan Stanley & Co., Incorporated, New York: March 1985 in R. Platt (ed.), *Controlling Interest Rate Risk*, New York: Wiley, 1986.

Bradley, Michael, "The Economic Consequences of Mergers and Tender Offers," *Midland Corporate Finance Journal*, Winter 1983.

Clark, W., and M. Weinstein, "The Behavior of Common Stock of Bankrupt Firms," *Journal of Finance*, May 1983.

Drexel Burnham Lambert, *High Yield Newsletter*, Los Angeles, Bimonthly, 1982–1986.

Drexel Burnham Lambert. *The Case for High Yield Bonds*, Los Angeles, 1984, 1985.

Dym, Steven, and K. Garbade, "Duration: An Introduction to the Concepts and Its Uses," *Topics in Money & Securities Markets*, Bankers Trust Co., New York, January 1984.

Fitzpatrick, J.D., and J.T. Severiens, "Hickman Revisited: The Case for Junk Bonds," *Journal of Portfolio Management*, Vol. 4, No. 4, Summer 1978.

Flynn, Thomas J., "Columbia Savings & Loan Rolls On," *High Performance*, Morgan Stanley & Co., Incorporated, July 1985.

Forsyth, Randall W., "Bad Grades: Takeovers Teach a Costly Lesson to Bond Holders," *Barrons*, February 24, 1986.

Fridson, Martin S., "Credit Trends and Returns—1985," *High Performance*, Morgan Stanley & Co., Incorporated, New York, March 1986: pp. 2–9.

Fridson, Martin S., and Marocco, Michael A., "Section on Financial Statement Analysis" in E.I. Altman (ed.), *Handbook of Corporate Finance*, New York: Wiley, 1986.

Fridson, Martin S., and Wahl, Fritz, "Plain Talk About Takeovers," *High Performance*, Morgan Stanley & Co., Incorporated, New York, February 1986.

Grimm & Co., W.T., *Mergers & Acquisitions Review 1984*, W.T. Grimm & Co., 1984.

Hickman, W.B., *Corporate Bond Quality and Investor Experience*, Princeton University Press and the National Bureau of Economic Research, 1958.

Hill, J.H., and L.A. Post, "The 1977–78 Lower-Rated Debt Market: Selectivity, High Yields, Opportunity," *Smith Barney Harris Upham & Co.*, December 1978.

Lipper-Fixed Income Fund Performance, Lipper Analytical Services Corp., New York, December 31, 1985, March 31, 1986, April 30, 1986.

Macauley, F., "Some Theoretical Problems Suggested by the Movements of Interest Rates, Bond Yields and Stock Prices in the U.S. Since 1856," *NBER*, 1938.

Moody's Inc., "Rating Changes and Debt Offerings," *Moody's Bond Survey*, January 27, 1986.

Paulus, John D., "Corporate Restructuring, 'Junk' and Leverage: Too Much or Too Little," Morgan Stanley & Co., Incorporated, New York, March 12, 1986.

Platt, Robert, ed., *Controlling Interest Rate Risk*, New York: Wiley, 1986.

Pension and Investments Age, January 20, 1986.

Securities and Exchange Commission, "Noninvestment Grade Debt as Source of Tender Offer Financing," Office of Chief Economist, Wash. DC, June 20, 1986.

Siegel, S., *Non-Parametric Statistics*, New York: McGraw-Hill, 1956.

Soldofsky, R., "Risk and Return for Long Term Securities: 1971–1982," *Journal of Portfolio Management*, Fall 1984.

Standard & Poor's, "Corporate Debt Default Risk," *Credit Comment*, February 20, 1984.

Standard & Poor's, "Corporate Downgrades Set Record," *Standard & Poor's Credit Week, January 16, 1986.*

Standard & Poor's Inc., *Credit Watch*, 1985, 1986.

Standard & Poor's, *Bond Guide*, monthly.

Toevs, Alden L., and William C. Haney, "Measuring and Managing Interest Rate Risk: A Guide to Asset/Liability Models Used in Banks and Thrifts," Morgan Stanley & Co., Incorporated, New York, October 1984.

Wahl, F., and Martin S. Fridson, "Quality Trends of Seasonal Issues," Morgan Stanley & Co., Incorporated, New York, July 1985.

Weisenberger Investment Company Services, New York, a division of Warren Gorham & Lamont, Boston, MA, 1984, 1985.

Wilcoxon, F., and F. Wilcox, *Some Rapid Approximate Statistical Pro-*

cedures, Lederle Laboratories, American Cyanamid, Pearl River, NY, 1964 revised.

Zeta Services Inc., "Analysis Book," Hoboken, NJ, 1984, 1985.

Zeta Services, Inc., "Company Credit Reports," Hoboken, NJ, 1978–1986.

Index

Printed in the United States
58083LVS00003B/131

9 781587 981555